Microsoft® PowerPoint 97

Short Course

Iris Blanc
Jennifer Frew

Acknowledgements

Alan, Pamela, and Jaime–*I.B.*
Michael–J.F.

Specials thanks to Shu Chen for doing an amazing job on the layout.

Managing Editor	Technical and English Editors	Design and Layout
Jennifer Frew New York, NY	Rebecca Fiala Quincy, MA	Shu Chen New York, NY
	Aegina Berg New York, NY	Christine Ford New York, NY

Contents

Lesson 3: Work with Slide Shows

Lesson 4: Charts and Tables

ABOUT THIS BOOK

PowerPoint 97 for Windows *95* Short Course enables you to master the most commonly used features of PowerPoint 97 on an IBM PC or compatible computer. Each lesson in this book will explain PowerPoint concepts, provide exercises to apply those concepts, and illustrate the necessary keystrokes or mouse actions to complete the exercises. Summary exercises are provided to challenge and reinforce the concepts you have learned.

After completing all of the exercises in this book, you will be able to use PowerPoint 97 for Windows 95 with ease.

FEATURES OF THIS TEXT

- Lesson Objectives
- Exercise Objectives
- PowerPoint 97 concepts and vocabulary
- A Log of Exercises which lists exercise and data/solutions disk file names in exercise order
- A directory of Documents which lists file names alphabetically along with the exercise number in which each was used
- End-of-Lesson summary exercises to reinforce what you have learned and to test your knowledge of lesson concepts
- Mouse actions or keystrokes necessary to complete each exercise
- A data disk that eliminates the need to keyboard lengthy text. If you choose not to use the data disk, you may create the exercises as directed. Each data file is named using a descriptive name, an exercise number, and is preceded by a ⊞ symbol (example: ⊞**11MAGAZINE**).

   ✓ *If you are saving files to a network drive, filenames can only be eight characters long.*

HOW TO USE THIS BOOK

Each exercise contains four parts:
- Notes: Explain PowerPoint concepts being introduced. Graphic symbols to call your attention to:

 Quick feature access

 Tips for using a feature or completing an exercise

 Cautions and warnings

- Exercise Directions: Tell you how to complete the exercise.
- Exercises: Let you apply the concept that was introduced.
- Keystroke/Mouse Actions: Outline the keystrokes or mouse actions needed to complete the exercise.

   ✓ *The mouse actions and keystrokes are provided only when a new concept is introduced. If you forget the keystroke/mouse procedures to complete a task, you can use the Help feature (explained in Exercise 2) or you can look the procedure up in the Index.*

SOLUTIONS/INSTRUCTOR'S GUIDE ON DISK

While this text can be used as a self-paced learning book, a comprehensive Instructor's Guide is available on disk. The Instructor's Guide contains the following:
- Lesson objectives
- Exercise objectives
- Related vocabulary
- Points to emphasize
- Exercise settings

Since the Instructor's Guide is on disk, teachers may print all or only those sections they desire to plan their lessons. Pages may be used as the teacher's actual lesson plan.

The solutions on disk may be used to compare your work with the final solution.

The Instructor's Guide and solutions disk may be purchased from the publisher.

Log of Exercises

Lesson	Exercise	Filename	Data file	Solution file	Page
1	1	WPRT	-	S01WPRT	10
		MAGAZINE	-	S01MAGAZ	10
	2	WPRT	02WPRT	S02WPRT	23
		MAGAZINE	02MAGAZINE	S02MAGAZ	23
	3	WPRT	03WPRT	S03WPRT	30
		MAGAZINE	03MAGAZINE	S03MAGAZ	31
	4	WPRT	04WPRT	S04WPRT	36
	5	SWITZERLAND	-	S05SWITZ	43
	6	OLYMPIC	-	S06OLYMP	44
	7	EGYPT	-	S07EGYPT	46
2	8	WPRT	08WPRT	S08WPRT	55
	9	SWITZERLAND	09SWIT	S09SWITZ	63
	10	PUZZLE	-	S10PUZZLE.pot	72
		EFFECT	-	S10EFFEC	72
	11	WPRT	11WPRT	S11WPRT	80
	12	BOUNCE	-	S12BOUNC.pot	84
		WPRT	12WPRT	S12WPRT	84
	13	VACATION	-	S14VACAT	88
3	14	EFFECT	14EFFECT	S14EFFEC	97
	15	VACATION	15VACATI	S15VACAT	105
	16	WPRT	16WPRT	S16WPRT	108
	17	VACATION	17VACATI	S17VACAT	113
	18	MINUTES	-	S18MINUT	120
	19	EFFECT	19EFFECT	S19EFFEC	122
	20	WPRT	20WPRT	S20WPRT	123
4	21	INVEST	-	S21INVES	128
	22	SWITZERLAND	22SWIT	S22SWITZ	133
	23	INVEST	23INVEST	S23INVES	140
	24	VACATION	24VACATI	S24VACAT	144
	25	MINUTES	25MINUTES	S25MINUT	145

Directory of Documents

Exercise(s)	Filename	Page(s)
12	BOUNCE	84
10, 14, 19	EFFECT	72, 97, 122
7	EGYPT	46
4, 21	INVEST	128, 140
1, 2, 3	MAGAZINE	10, 23, 31
5, 18	MINUTES	120, 145
6	OLYMPIC	44
10	PUZZLE	72
5, 9, 22	SWITZERLAND	43, 63, 133
4, 13, 15, 17	VACATION	88, 105, 113, 144
1, 2, 3, 4, 8, 12, 16, 20	WPRT	10, 23, 30, 36, 55, 80, 84, 108, 123

Lesson 1

Create, Save, and Print a Presentation
Exercises 1-7

- About PowerPoint
- Start PowerPoint
- The Blank Presentation Option
- Use the Template Option
- Add Slides to a Presentation
- Add Text to Placeholders
- Save a Presentation
- Save File as HTML
- Exit PowerPoint
- Open a Presentation
- Slide Views
- Print
- Spell Checking
- Office Assistant
- Work with Object Slides
- Use Undo and Redo
- Change a Slide's Layout or Template
- Move, Copy, Duplicate, and Delete Slides
- Slide Sorter View

Exercise

1

■ About PowerPoint ■ Start PowerPoint ■ Create a Presentation Using the Blank Presentation Option ■ The PowerPoint Screen ■ Create a Presentation Using the Template Option ■ Add Text to Placeholders ■ Add Slides to a Presentation ■ Save a Presentation ■ Save File as HTML ■ Close a Presentation/Exit PowerPoint

NOTES

About PowerPoint

■ PowerPoint is the presentation graphics component of Microsoft Office that lets you create, save, and run presentations.

■ A **presentation** is a collection of slides relating to the same topic that may be shown while an oral report is given to help summarize data and emphasize report highlights. From the presentation slides, you can prepare handouts for the audience, speaker notes for use during the presentation, or outlines to provide an overview of the presentation. In addition, you can use slides as a table of contents or as overhead transparencies. You can also create 35 mm slides of your presentation.

■ PowerPoint slides may include text, drawings, charts, outlines, graphics, video, and/or audio clips.

■ Outlines created in Word, or data created in Access or Excel, can be imported into a PowerPoint slide. A PowerPoint slide may be imported into a Word document.

Start PowerPoint

■ PowerPoint may be started using any one of the following procedures:

• Using the Windows 95 Taskbar: Click *Start*, highlight *Programs*, highlight and select *Microsoft PowerPoint*.

• Using the Windows 95 Taskbar: Click *Start*, highlight and select *New Office Document*. Click *Blank Presentation*, or click the *Presentation Designs* tab, select a presentation design, and click OK.

• Using the Office Shortcut bar: Click *New Office Document,* and click *Blank Presentation* (or click the *Presentation Designs* tab), select a presentation design, and click OK.

To start PowerPoint 97 using the Taskbar:

• Click **Start** on the Taskbar.

• Highlight **Programs**.

• Highlight and select **Microsoft PowerPoint**.

• Click **Blank Presentation**.

• Click **OK**.

  OR

• Click **Start** on the Taskbar.

• Highlight and select **New Office Document**.

• Click **Blank Presentation**.

• Click **OK**.

- If you launch PowerPoint using the first method, the following PowerPoint dialog box appears and presents options to create a new presentation, using one of three methods (AutoContent wizard, Template, or Blank Presentation), or you may choose to Open an existing presentation. One of the options uses an AutoContent wizard. Wizards walk you through the presentation development process.

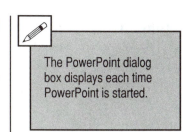

The PowerPoint dialog box displays each time PowerPoint is started.

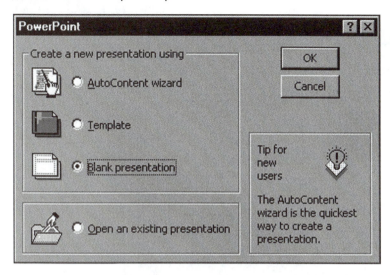

- If you launch PowerPoint using methods two or three, you will have the option of creating a blank presentation or using a template design. Select the appropriate tab and option in the New Office Document dialog box.

Click the Presentations tab to display predesigned presentations.

Click the General tab to select the Blank Presentation icon.

Click the Presentation Designs tab to display all available templates.

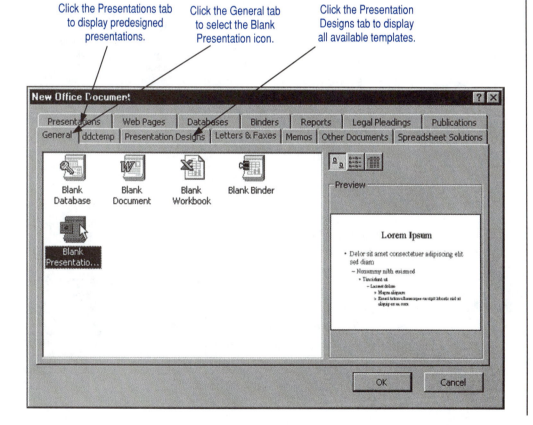

Create a Presentation Using the Blank Presentation Option

■ The Blank Presentation option lets you build your own unique presentation from blank slides which contain standard default formats and layouts.

■ After you select a Blank Presentation and click OK, the New Slide dialog box appears.

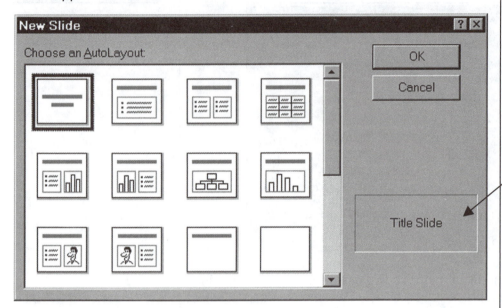

Selected slide layout identification box

■ The New Slide dialog box includes a set of 24 different AutoLayout formats that arrange various types of objects on slides. Objects include titles, charts, graphics, or bulleted lists—standard objects that you might want to place on a slide.

■ AutoLayout formats follow the natural progression of your presentation. They start with a Title Slide format and move to more complex layouts.

■ The name of each AutoLayout appears in the box at the lower-right corner of the New Slide dialog box when that design is selected. Select a slide layout which is appropriate to the data you are presenting. The Title Slide is the default setting for the first slide in every presentation.

■ After you select an AutoLayout and click OK, the PowerPoint screen appears.

The PowerPoint Screen

■ PowerPoint places the generic title *Presentation* in the **Title bar** of each presentation you create.

■ The **Standard toolbar** contains many buttons that appear in the other Office 97 applications, but it also includes buttons unique to PowerPoint. Each button will be presented when it is relevant to an exercise.

■ The **Drawing toolbar**, located above the Status bar at the bottom of the screen, contains some of the most common tools used to add illustrations to slides.

Many of the AutoLayout slide formats have placeholders for inserting clip art, charts, and even video clips.

In later exercises, you will learn to rearrange objects and design your own layouts so that the slides become more suitable for your needs.

You will note that many of the PowerPoint tools, such as the Formatting and Standard toolbars, are similar in appearance and function to tools in other Office 97 applications.

- The **Common Tasks toolbar** is displayed when you open a new presentation. Several of the most common functions are available on this toolbar.

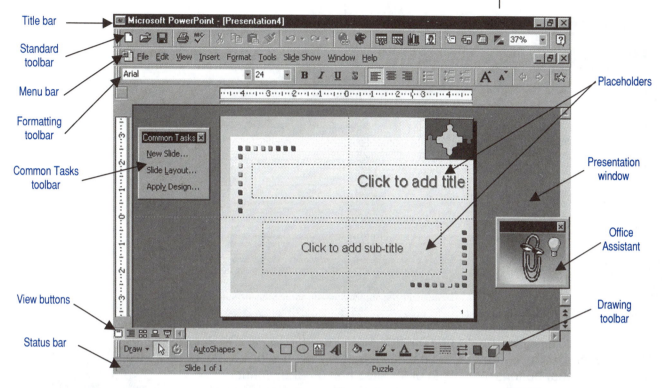

- The **Office Assistant** appears when you first open a PowerPoint presentation. *(See page 21 for more on the Office Assistant.)*

- **View buttons**, located at the bottom of the Presentation window, above the Status bar, control the number of slides PowerPoint displays and the display layout. *(Views will be covered in Exercise 2.)*

- The **Status bar**, located at the bottom of the PowerPoint window, contains information and buttons that makes performing the most common tasks more efficient:

Slide number	Identifies the slide currently displayed.
Template name	Identifies the template design name.
Spell Check Indicator	Indicates if Automatic Spell Check is on or off.

> Although each toolbar has a default location on the PowerPoint screen, any toolbar can be dragged to a new location, resized, or hidden (View, Toolbar).

Create a Presentation Using the Template Option

- The **Template** option lets you create slides with a predesigned format. PowerPoint provides over 100 professionally designed formats with colorful backgrounds and text from which you can choose.

- After you select Template in the PowerPoint dialog box and click OK, a New Presentation dialog box appears. To select a template design, click the Presentation Designs tab. Each template is displayed by a large icon. (You can also display templates in List and Details views by clicking the appropriate button.)

> In Exercise 10, you will learn to create and save your own templates.
>
> Templates that you create are stored on the General tab, not the Presentation Designs tab.

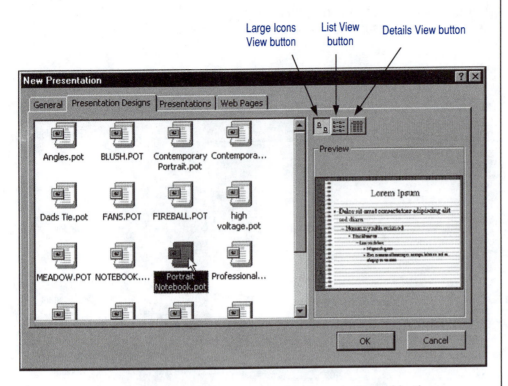

- Templates for designing online presentations are included in the Presentation Designs group. The designs of these presentations suggest the placement of buttons for links to other sites and other elements commonly used to create a web page for the Word Wide Web. These designs can also be used for creating a slide presentation if you wish.

- After you select the template design you desire and click OK, select an AutoLayout from the New Slide dialog box and click OK once again. The PowerPoint screen appears.

- PowerPoint also provides a content templates that contain predesigned formats and suggestions for a specific type of presentation. For example, suppose you wanted to report the status of a project. PowerPoint includes a ten-slide presentation with suggestions for titles and bulleted information. To access specific slide presentations, click the Presentations tab in the New or New Presentations dialog box.

PowerPoint 97 includes numerous content templates.

These templates provide ideas, organization, and starter text in addition to the formatting found in regular templates. These templates cover a wide variety of topics. PowerPoint 97 also includes templates from Dale Carnegie Training that provide presentation tips.

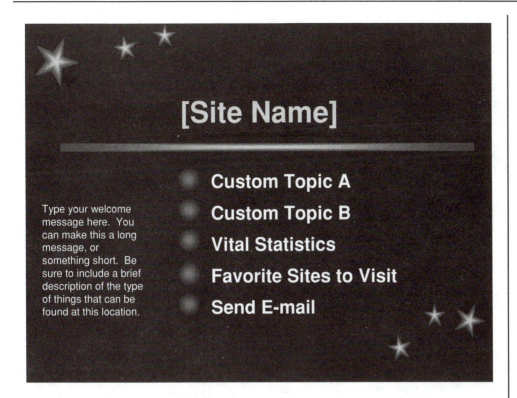

Add Text to Placeholders

- PowerPoint displays slides with **placeholders** (an empty box or boxes) which identify the placement and location of objects on a slide. Each placeholder contains directions to help you complete a slide.

- Whether you select the Blank Presentation or Template option, **title placeholders** contain a format for title text while **body text placeholders** include a format and design for subtitles or bulleted lists.

- To type text into a placeholder, click inside the placeholder and note the handles that appear. Enter the text as prompted.

If you start typing without selecting the text placeholder, PowerPoint automatically places the text in the first text placeholder.

PowerPoint also automatically capitalizes the first letter of any text entered in a new presentation. To keep text in lowercase, simply correct the text and it will not be changed again within that presentation.

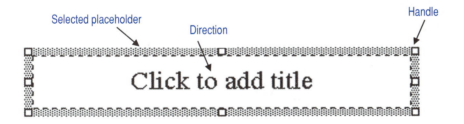

Add Slides to a Presentation

- To add a new slide to the presentation, click the New Slide button on the Standard toolbar. The New Slide dialog box appears, allowing you to select an AutoLayout for the new slide.

New Slide button

- The Bulleted List format is automatically selected (but need not be chosen and used) when you add a second slide to a presentation.

- Five different bulleted sub-levels are available for slides with bulleted lists. Pressing Tab indents text and produces sub levels of bulleted items. Different bullet shapes identify the tab levels, and the text size gets smaller with each sub level. Pressing Shift+Tab returns you to the previous bullet level.

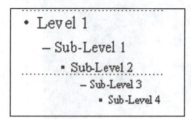

- PowerPoint places the new slide immediately after the slide that is displayed or selected at the time you create the new slide.

Save a Presentation

- Presentations must be given a name for identification. A filename may contain a maximum of 255 characters, can include spaces, and is automatically assigned the extension .PPT. If you are working on a network, however, filenames can have only eight characters and the names cannot include spaces.

- You can create, display, and edit summary information by selecting Properties from the File menu. In the Presentation Properties dialog box, under the Summary tab, you can add key words, a presentation title, comments, and other information you want to save with the file. *(See illustration below.)*

- To see a statistics summary of your presentation, select the Statistics tab.

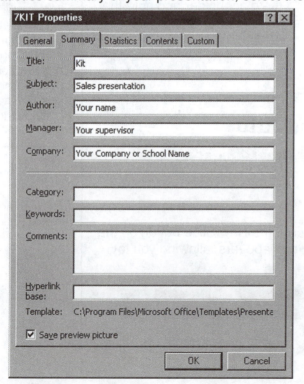

In Exercise 4, you will learn how to move slides to a different sequence in a presentation.

Save File as HTML

- Presentations created in PowerPoint can be saved in HTML format (**Hypertext Markup Language**) for publishing on the World Wide Web. When you select Save File as <u>H</u>TML on the <u>F</u>ile menu, the Internet Wizard (illustrated below) appears.

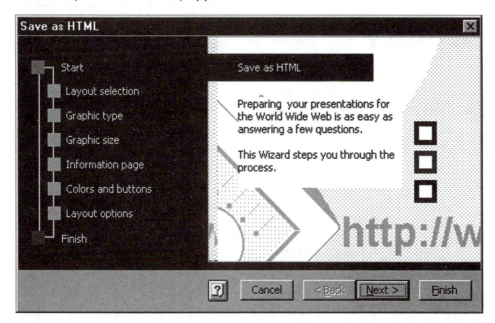

- The Internet Wizard will walk you through the steps for creating an online presentation. Settings created for an online presentation can be saved and reused for other presentations.

Close a Presentation/Exit PowerPoint

- When a presentation has been saved, it remains on your screen. If you wish to clear the screen, you may close the presentation window by selecting <u>C</u>lose from the <u>F</u>ile menu or by double-clicking the Document Control icon.

- If you attempt to close a presentation before saving it, PowerPoint will prompt you to save it before exiting. You may respond **Y** for Yes or **N** for No.

- If you make a mistake and would like to begin the presentation again, close the presentation without saving it.

Save file as HTML
- Click **File**.
- Click **Save as HTML**.
- Make appropriate selections in the Wizard dialog boxes.
- Click **Finish** when complete.

For more information about creating HTML files, open the Help menu, select Microsoft on the Web, and then click Product News.

PowerPoint follows the same procedures for closing a file and exiting as in the Word, Access, and Excel application tools.

If the presentation you are working on has been modified or has not yet been saved, you will be prompted to save it.

In Part I of this exercise, you will create a presentation using a title slide and bulleted list slide using the Blank Presentation option. In Part II of this exercise, you will create a presentation using a title and bulleted list slide using the Template option. You will save both presentations.

EXERCISE DIRECTIONS

PART I

1. Start PowerPoint using the Windows Taskbar (highlight Programs), and create a new blank presentation.

2. Accept the default Title Slide AutoLayout for the first slide.

3. Type the title and subtitle as shown in Illustration A on the next page.

4. Click the New Slide button and accept the default, bulleted–list slide for the second slide.

5. Type the heading and the bulleted list as shown in Illustration A.

6. Save the presentation; name it **WPRT**.

7. Fill in the summary information as follows:

   Title: (Accept the default)
   Subject: Management Meeting
   Author: Your name
   Manager: Your supervisor or teacher's name
   Company: Your company or school name
   Category: Management
   Keywords: Forecast, projections

8. Close the presentation window and save the changes.

PART II

1. Create a new template presentation using the **Zesty** template.

2. Accept the default Title Slide layout for the first slide and the bulleted list slide for the second slide.

3. Type the title and bulleted list slides shown in Illustration B on the next page.

4. Save the presentation; name it **MAGAZINE**.

5. Fill in the summary information as follows:

   Title: (Accept the default)
   Subject: Company Introduction
   Author: Your Name
   Manager: Your supervisor or teacher's name
   Company: Your company or school name
   Category: Sales
   Keywords: Strategy

6. Close the presentation window and save the changes.

ILLUSTRATION A

WPRT Television

Management Team
Annual Meeting

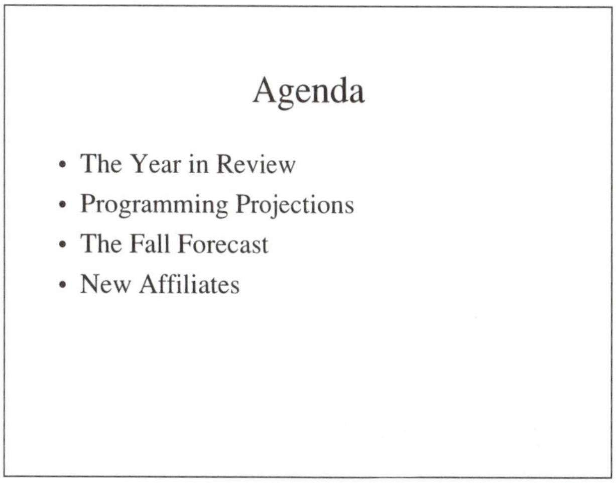

Agenda

- The Year in Review
- Programming Projections
- The Fall Forecast
- New Affiliates

ILLUSTRATION B

Internet Magazine

Marketing Strategy

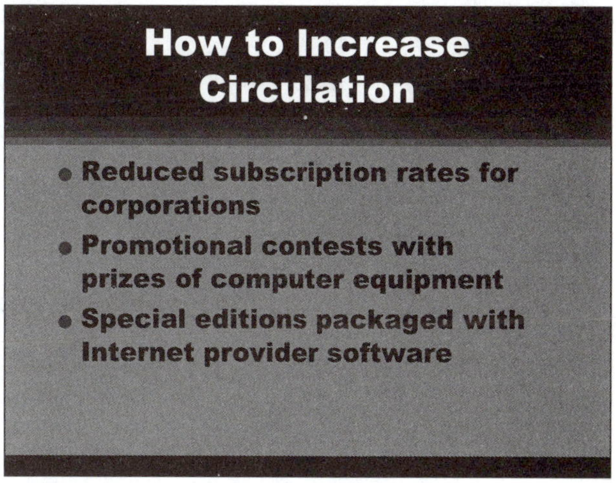

How to Increase Circulation

- Reduced subscription rates for corporations
- Promotional contests with prizes of computer equipment
- Special editions packaged with Internet provider software

KEYSTROKES

START POWERPOINT

Using the Taskbar

1. Click **Start** .... `Ctrl` + `Esc`

2. Click **Programs** .... `P`

3. Select **Microsoft PowerPoint.**

   OR

1. Click **Start** .... `Ctrl` + `Esc`

2. Select **New Office Document** ....

3. Double-click **Blank** .... **Presentation** to create a blank presentation.

   OR

   a. Click Presentation Designs tab.

   b. Select a template design to create a designed presentation.

   c. Click **OK** .... `Enter`

4. Highlight bulleted text and replace with new text.

Using the Office Shortcut Bar

1. Click **New Office Document** button ....

2. Double-click  to create a blank presentation.

   OR

   a. Click presentation Designs tab.

   b. Select a template design to create a designed presentation.

3. Click **OK** .... `Enter`

SAVE PRESENTATION

Ctrl + S

1. Click **Save** button ....

   OR

   a. Click **File** .... `Alt` + `F`

   b. Click **Save** .... `S`

2. Click **Save in** text box .... `Alt` + `I`

3. Select desired .... `↓` , `Enter` drive or folder.

   To select subfolder, if necessary:
   Double-click folder .... `Tab` , `↓` , `Enter`

4. Click **File name** .... `Alt` + `N` text box.

5. Type presentation name .... *filename*

6. Click **Save** .... `S`

   ✓ *Saved presentation files will be assigned the extension .PPT.*

SAVE FILE AS HTML

1. Click **File** .... `F`

2. Click **Save as HTML** .... `H`

3. Make appropriate selections in the Wizard dialog boxes.

4. Click **Finish** .... `Alt` + `F` when complete.

To Save HTML conversion settings for later use:

   a. Type a name for the settings in the text box.

   b. Click **Save** .... `Alt` + `S`

■ **Open a Presentation** ■ **PowerPoint Views** ■ **Display Slides**
■ **Spell Checking** ■ **Print a Presentation** ■ **Help Features**
■ **Help Topics Window** ■ **Screen Tips** ■ **Office Assistant** ■ **Exit Help**

NOTES

Open a Presentation

■ Presentations may be opened by selecting **Open an existing presentation** from the PowerPoint dialog box, or by selecting <u>O</u>pen from the <u>F</u>ile menu.

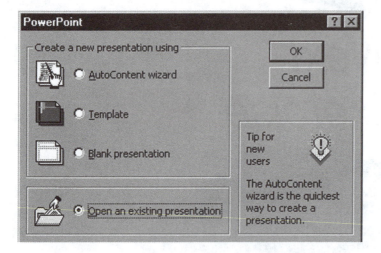

PowerPoint Views

■ PowerPoint lets you view your presentation in five different ways.

■ Views may be changed by clicking the appropriate view button on the bottom left of the presentation window or by selecting the desired view from the <u>V</u>iew menu.

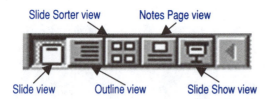

Slide Sorter view   Notes Page view

Slide view   Outline view   Slide Show view

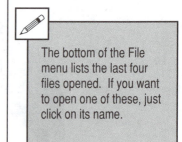

The bottom of the File menu lists the last four files opened. If you want to open one of these, just click on its name.

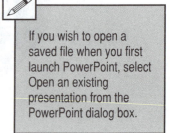

If you wish to open a saved file when you first launch PowerPoint, select Open an existing presentation from the PowerPoint dialog box.

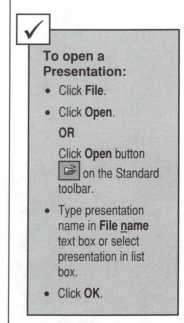

To open a Presentation:

• Click **File**.

• Click **Open**.

 OR

 Click **Open** button
 on the Standard toolbar.

• Type presentation name in **File name** text box or select presentation in list box.

• Click **OK**.

- **Slide view**, the default, allows you to see a single slide on screen. You edit or modify a slide in this view.

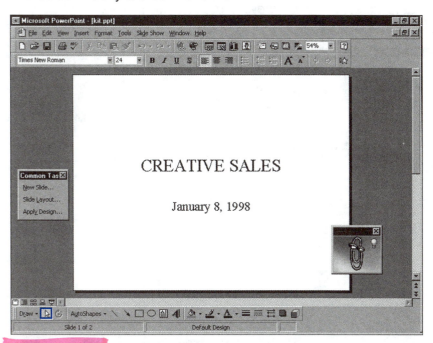

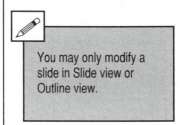

You may only modify a slide in Slide view or Outline view.

- **Outline view** displays slide text in a notebook page layout to give an overview of the contents of a presentation. Use this view to organize a presentation. *(This view will be detailed in Exercise 5.)*

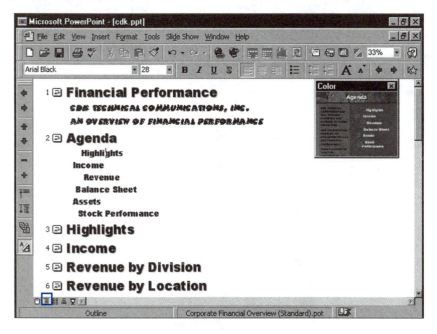

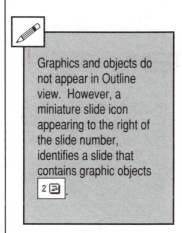

Graphics and objects do not appear in Outline view. However, a miniature slide icon appearing to the right of the slide number, identifies a slide that contains graphic objects.

- **Slide Sorter view** lets you see miniature copies of your slides on screen so you can see the flow of the presentation. Use this view to move, copy, duplicate, and delete slides. *(Moving, copying, duplicating, and deleting slides will be detailed in Exercise 4.)*

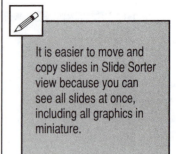

It is easier to move and copy slides in Slide Sorter view because you can see all slides at once, including all graphics in miniature.

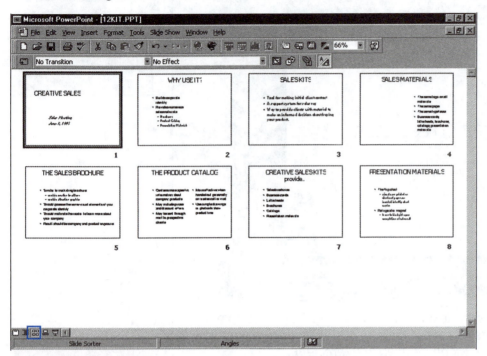

- **Notes Page view** lets you display speaker's note pages for each slide. *(This view will be detailed in a later exercise.)*

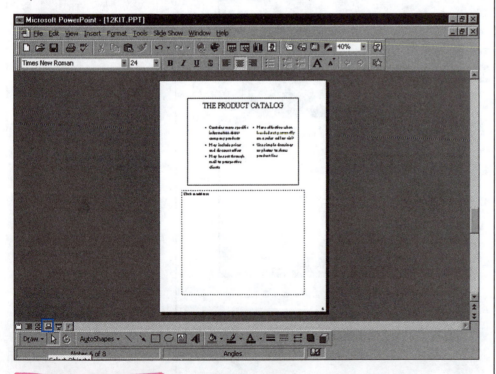

- **Slide Show view** lets you see your slides as an on-screen presentation. *(This view will be detailed in a later exercise.)*

■ **Black and White view** allows you to see what your presentation will look like in black and white. Select **Black and White** from the Ⅴiew menu. If Slide Mⅰniature is selected on the Ⅴiew menu, a color version of the slide will appear in Slide, Notes, and Outline views when this option is selected. To return to color view, Select Ⅴlack and White from the Ⅴiew menu again.

Display Slides

■ When there are a number of slides included in a presentation, you will find it necessary to move from slide to slide to edit, enhance, or view the slide information. PowerPoint offers a variety of ways to select and display slides in Slide view:

• Press PgDn to display the next slide, or PgUp to display the previous slide.

• Click the **Next Slide** or **Previous Slide** button on the vertical slide scroll bar.

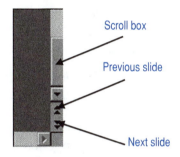

Scroll box

Previous slide

Next slide

• Drag the vertical slide scroll box up or down until the desired slide number is displayed.

Spell Checking

■ If AutoCorrect spell checking is activated, wavy red lines appear under words that PowerPoint recognizes as possible errors.
To disable AutoCorrect:

• Click Options on the Ⅰools menu.

• Select the Spelling tab.

• Deselect Spelling check box.

OR

Click Hide spelling errors check box.

✓ *Note: When you finish your presentation, you can deselect the Hide spelling errors check box and verify the words that have been identified as potential errors.*

■ After creating your presentation, click the Spelling button on the Standard toolbar or select Spelling from the Ⅰools menu or press F7.

The Black and White view is used to conserve system resources, or to see how a presentation looks without color formatting. This feature is useful if you are printing slides as handouts and do not have a color printer.

To Spell Check:
• Click **Spelling** button on the standard toolbar.

OR

• Click **Tools**.
• Click **Spelling**.

Be careful. Many words will match a spell check definition but may not be the correct spelling for a particular usage. For example, *there* is used for *their*.

Spell Check will not see the word as incorrect and will skip over it. However, the usage error will remain in your document.

Print a Presentation

- Slides in your presentation may be used as an on-screen show, transparencies, 35mm slides, notes pages, handouts, or as an outline. Therefore, you must specify certain setup information, depending on how you wish to use the slides or printouts. Select Page Setup from the File menu, and indicate your print specifications in the Page Setup dialog box that follows.

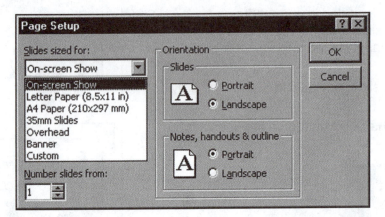

- Printing PowerPoint slides is similar to printing pages in a Word document and worksheets in an Excel workbook. To print PowerPoint slides, select Print from the File menu, or press Ctrl+P. In the Print dialog box that follows, you may print the active slide, a selected slide range, or all slides in a presentation. When you print all slides of a presentation, each slide prints on a separate page. The Print what feature lets you indicate whether you want your presentation printed as slides, notes pages, handouts (with 2, 3, or 6 slides per page), or as an outline. *(Notes pages and handouts will be detailed in Exercise 17.)*

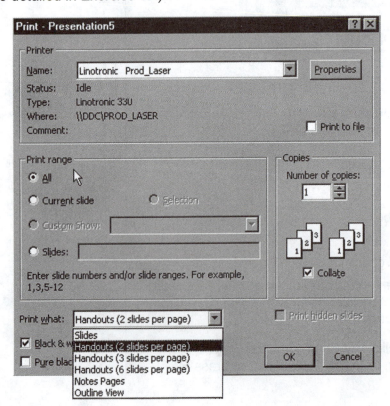

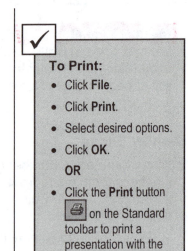

To Print:
- Click **File**.
- Click **Print**.
- Select desired options.
- Click **OK**.
  OR
- Click the **Print** button on the Standard toolbar to print a presentation with the default print settings.

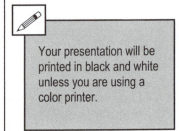

Your presentation will be printed in black and white unless you are using a color printer.

- You can also click the **Print** button 🖨 on the Standard toolbar. When you use the Print button, however, you bypass the Print dialog box and send the Print command directly to the printer. PowerPoint automatically prints information using the settings last selected in the Print dialog box.

- The default selection in the Print dialog box prints all slides. Other options are listed in the table below:

Option	*Description*
Properties	Changes elements specific to the printer such as paper size, orientation, graphics, fonts, and so on.
Print to file	Prints the presentation to a disk file so that it may be sent to a service bureau for printing in an alternate format such as 35mm slides.
Collate copies	Prints multiple copies as collated sets.
Print hidden slides	Prints slides that have been hidden.
Black & white	Turns all color fills to white and adds a thin black frame to all unbordered objects without text. Use this option if you plan to use your slides as overhead transparencies or if you have a printer that only prints black and white.
Pure black & white	Prints in black and white without gray scale.
Scale to fit paper	Scales presentation slides to fit a custom or different sized paper.
Frame slides	Adds a frame to each slide when it is printed.
All	Prints all pages in the presentation. Default option when Print button is clicked on the Standard toolbar.
Current slide	Prints only the slide currently visible in slide view.
Slides	Prints only the slides entered in the text box. You may enter individual slide numbers or slide ranges.

Help Features

- Help is available from a variety of sources in PowerPoint. Below is an illustration of the Help features available on the PowerPoint Help menu.

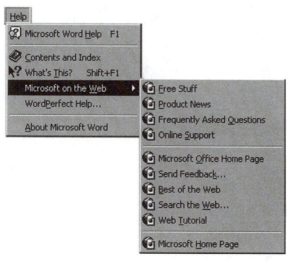

Help Topics Window

■ If you select **Contents and Index** on the Help menu, you will be able to use the Contents, Index, and/or the Find options to look for help.

Contents Tab

■ The Contents tab displays a page listing the Help Contents by topic in PowerPoint. Double-clicking on a topic presents a list of subtopics and/or display screens. Note the PowerPoint Contents page and the example of a display screen illustrated below.

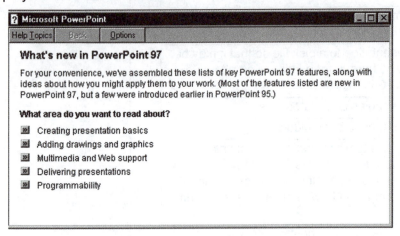

Index Tab

■ The Index tab allows you to enter the first few letters of your topic, then brings you to an index entry. Double-click the desired entry, or select it and click the Display button. The Help screen related to your topic is then displayed.

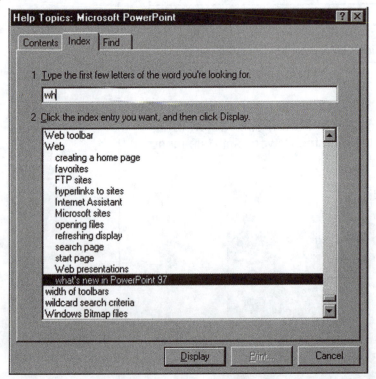

Find Tab

■ The Find tab accesses the Help database feature. It allows you to search the Help database for the occurrence of any word or phrase in a Help topic. The Index and Find features are similar; however, Find offers more options to search for a topic.

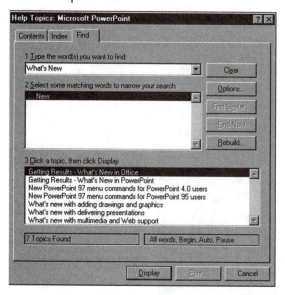

ScreenTips

■ You can find out information about screen elements by selecting the What's This? feature on the Help menu, then pointing to the element you want information about and clicking the mouse.
■ Or, you may click the question mark icon in the upper-right corner of any dialog box, and then click on the feature about which you want information.

Office Assistant

■ By default, the Office Assistant appears on screen when you open PowerPoint. The Office Assistant will answer questions, offer suggestions, and provide help unique to PowerPoint.
■ Click on the Assistant, type your question, and click the Search button. The suggested procedures display.

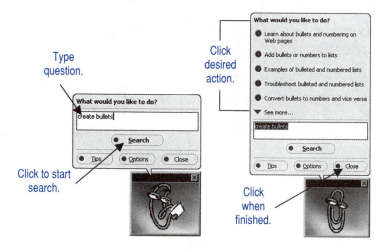

- You can control the way the Office Assistant appears on screen as well as the kind of information that it presents. You can also turn the Assistant off. If you turn the Assistant off, you can easily turn it on again by clicking the Office Assistant button 🔲 on the Standard toolbar.

- **To change the Assistant options:**
    - Click the Office Assistant (if it is on screen), or click the Office Assistant button on the toolbar.
    - Click the Options button.
    - Click the Options tab.
    - Select the desired options.

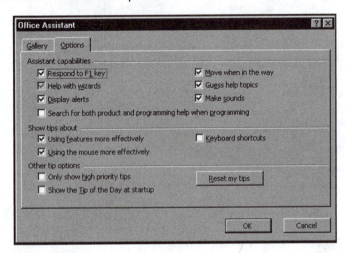

Select a Different Office Assistant

- The Gallery tab in the Office Assistant dialog box offers several different Assistant characters. After clicking the Gallery tab on the Office Assistant dialog box, click the Next and/or Back buttons to view the different Assistants. Click OK to select the desired assistant.

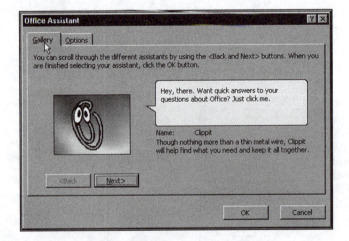

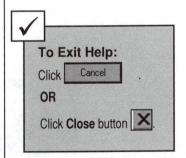

✓

To Exit Help:

Click ⬚Cancel⬚ .

OR

Click **Close** button ❎ .

Exit Help

- Click the Cancel or Close button, or press Escape to exit.

In this exercise, you will add new slides to previously created presentations. You will then use different slide views to see the flow of your presentation.

EXERCISE DIRECTIONS

PART I

1. Start PowerPoint using the Windows Taskbar and select Open an existing presentation from the PowerPoint dialog box.

    ✓ *If PowerPoint is already running, select File, Open to open a presentation.*

2. Open ⌨WPRT, or open 💾02WPRT.

3. Display slide 2 by clicking the Next Slide button.

4. Create a new bulleted list slide using the following information:

The Year in Review
• Organizational Changes
• Sales Records
• Ratings Review

    ✓ *The slide will be inserted after slide two. You will move it into another position in a later exercise.*

5. Switch to Slide Sorter view.

6. Switch back to Slide view.

7. Correct all spelling errors.

8. View your presentation in Black and White view.

9. In the Print dialog box, select Handouts with three slides per page as the Print what option. Print one copy in black and white.

10. Close the file; save the changes.

PART II

1. Open ⌨MAGAZINE, or open 💾02MAGAZINE

2. Display slide 2 using the PgDn key.

3. Display slide 1 using the PgUp key.

4. Create a new bulleted list slide using the following information:

Corporate Identity
• Prepare a logo and corporate image
• Use logo on all company-related materials:
• correspondence
• invoices
• price sheets

5. Switch to Slide Sorter view.

6. Switch to Slide view.

7. Correct all spelling errors.

8. View your presentation in Black and White and display the color slide in miniature.

9. Use the default print slide setup.

10. In the Print dialog box, select Handouts with three slides per page as the Print what option. Print one copy in black and white.

11. Close the file; save the changes.

KEYSTROKES

OPEN PRESENTATION

Ctrl + O

1. Click **File** .... `Alt`+`F`

2. Click **Open** .... `O`

   OR

   Click **Open** button 📂 on the Standard toolbar.

3. Type presentation name in **File name** text box .... *name* or select presentation in list box.

4. Click **OK** .... `Enter`

SPELL CHECK

F7

   Click **Spelling** 📝 button on the standard toolbar.

   OR

1. Click **Tools** .... `Alt`+`T`

2. Click **Spelling** .... `S`

   ✓ *If AutoCorrect is activated, wavy red lines will appear under misspelled words. To check the word(s), right-click on the word(s) in question and select the desired choice.*

SWITCH VIEWS

Select desired **View** button:

   🖼 **Slide** .... `Alt`+`V`, `S`

   📄 **Outline** .... `Alt`+`V`, `O`

   🔳 **Slide Sorter** .... `Alt`+`V`, `D`

   🖥 **Notes Page** .... `Alt`+`V`, `N`

   📽 **Slide Show** .... `Alt`+`V`, `W`

ADD SUBLEVELS

Press **Tab** to indent .... `Tab` text to next level.

   ✓ *Five different bulleted sublevels are available. Different bullet shapes identify the tab levels. Text size also gets smaller with each sublevel.*

OR

Press **Shift+Tab** .... `Shift`+`Tab`

to return to previous level

DISPLAY SLIDES

Press **PgUp** .... `Page Up` to display previous slide.

OR

Press **PgDn** .... `Page Down` to display next slide.

OR

Click **Next Slide** ⬇ or **Previous Slide** ⬆ button on scroll bar.

OR

Drag scroll box until desired slide is displayed.

PRINT PRESENTATION

Ctrl + P

1. Click **File** .... `Alt`+`F`

2. Click **Print** .... `P`

3. Select desired options.

4. Click **OK** .... `Esc`

   OR

   Click the **Print** button 🖨 on the Standard toolbar to print a presentation with the default print settings.

START OFFICE ASSISTANT

F1

   ✓ *By default, the Office Assistant will appear when you open PowerPoint. If the Assistant is not on screen however, you may use these steps to activate.*

Click **Office Assistant** button 📎 on the Standard toolbar.

   ✓ *If the Help Topics: Microsoft PowerPoint dialog box opens instead of the Office Assistant, the **respond to F1 key** check box option has been disabled in the Office Assistant: Options dialog box.*

CLOSE OFFICE ASSISTANT

Click **Close** button ❌ on Office Assistant.

USE OFFICE ASSISTANT

F1

1. Click **Office Assistant** button .... 📎

2. Type question in Assistant text box.

3. Click **Search** .... `Alt`+`S`

4. Select from list of procedures to view more information.

5. Press **Escape** .... `Esc` to close Help window.

CHANGE OFFICE ASSISTANT OPTIONS

1. Click **Office Assistant** .... `F1`

2. Click **Options** .... `Alt`+`O`

3. Click **Options** tab .... `Alt`+`O`

4. Select desired options.

5. Click **OK** .... `Enter`

USE HELP

1. Click **Help** .... `Alt`+`H`

2. Click **Contents and Index** .... `C`

3. Click the **Contents** tab.
   a. Double-click desired book or topic
   b. Double-click submenu item or display item.

   OR
   a. Click the Index tab.
   b. Type first letters of topic word in Step 1 text box.
   c. Double-click desired topic in Step 2 box.

   OR
   a. Select topic.
   b. Click **Display** .... `Alt`+`D`

   OR
   a. Click the **Find** tab.
   b. Type and enter a search word or phrase in Step 1 text box.
   c. Select matching words in Step 2, if presented.
   d. Double-click topic in Step 3 box.

   OR
   a. Select topic in Step 3 box.
   b. Click **Display** .... `D`

EXIT HELP

Click `Cancel` .... `Esc`

OR

Click **Close** button ❌.

Next
Exercise

- **Work with Object Slides** ■ **Use Undo and Redo**
- **Change a Slide's Layout or Template**

Insert Clip Art

Black and White View

Apply Design template

NOTES

Work with Object Slides

- In Exercise 1, you learned that a placeholder is an empty box that identifies the placement of objects on a slide. You entered text into placeholders for a title slide and a bulleted list slide. Some slides, however, also contain special placeholders to hold a particular type of item, like clip art, a graph, or a chart. Other slides contain an object placeholder that holds any type of object—text, clip art, a chart, or a media clip.

Clip Art
placeholder

Media Clip
placeholder

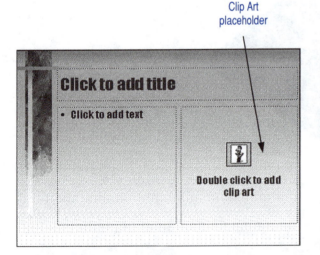

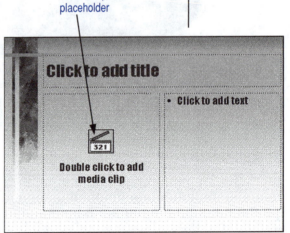

- When you select a slide layout containing a special placeholder, the placeholder itself contains directions prompting you to double-click within the placeholder to add the object. For example, if you are adding clip art, double-clicking the placeholder will open the Microsoft Clip Gallery, from which you can choose an image to insert into the clip art placeholder.

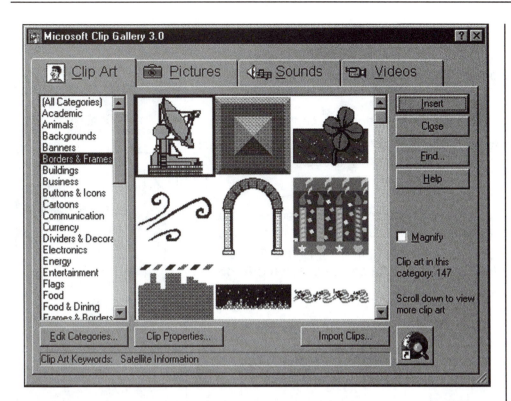

- You can also insert clip art by clicking on the Insert Clip Art button 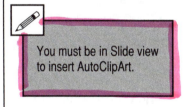 on the Standard toolbar.

- The AutoClipArt feature suggests relevant clip art based on the text you enter in your slides. To use AutoClipArt, select AutoClipArt from the Tools menu. The AutoClipArt dialog box that follows will display two drop-down list box arrows. Clicking the first drop-down list box arrow displays words in your presentation for which PowerPoint has found a relevant picture(s). The **On Slide** text box displays the slide number where the word has been entered. Select the word and slide number where you wish to add a suggested picture.

- To view the suggested picture(s), click the View Clip Art button. The Microsoft Clip Gallery opens and displays the picture(s) that best relate to the slide's text. However, you might find that the picture(s) selected by PowerPoint are not ones you desire. Remember, PowerPoint is only suggesting ideas.

> You must be in Slide view to insert AutoClipArt.

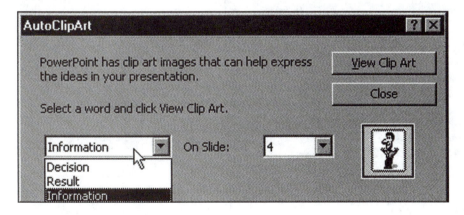

> AutoClipArt will only find clipart that relates to certain terms. If you enter a word AutoClipArt doesn't recognize, it will not find matching clips, but that does not mean that relevant clip art is not available. Try using the Find feature in Clip Gallery.

Undo

- The **Undo** feature lets you undo the last change you made to the document. PowerPoint allows you to undo 150 of the last actions completed.

- You can undo actions by clicking the **Undo** button on the Standard toolbar by clicking the **Undo** list arrow next to the Undo button to select the action(s) you wish to undo from the drop-down list box.

Redo

- The **Redo** feature allows you to reverse the last Undo procedure. Like Undo, Redo allows you to replace up to 150 deleted actions in documents. You can redo an action by clicking the **Redo** button on the Standard toolbar. And, as with the Undo procedure, you can also click the **Redo** list arrow next to the Redo button to select the action(s) you wish to redo from the Redo drop-down list box.

Change a Slide's Layout

- The layout or template of a slide may be changed at any time. If you have objects on the slide when you change the layout, they will not be lost, only rearranged.

- Use Slide view when changing a Slide's layout or template.

- To change the layout, click the Slide Layout button on the Standard toolbar, or select Slide Layout from the Format menu. The Slide Layout dialog box appears, letting you make another layout selection.

Change a Slide's Template

- Templates are predesigned presentations with a wide variety of stylish designs (background, font colors, object formatting). PowerPoint provides numerous professionally designed templates to choose from.

- Templates are organized by type and saved in the Presentation Designs subdirectory (folder) within the Templates subdirectory of the Microsoft Office directory.

- As you select a template from the list box, a preview of the template design appears in the right side of the dialog box

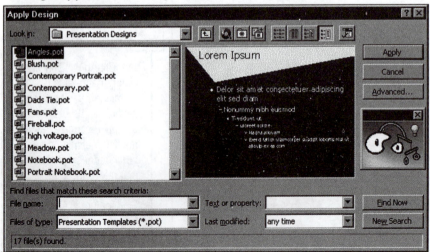

Certain actions, especially those that involve navigating through or saving a presentation, cannot be undone.

To change a Slide's Layout:

- Click **Slide Layout** button on Standard toolbar.

  OR

- Click **Format**.

- Click **Slide Layout**.

- Select a desired layout.

- Click **Apply**.

  OR

  Click **Reapply**.

To Change a Slide's Template:

- Click **Apply Design** button on Standard toolbar.

  OR

- Double-click template name on Status bar (Angles.pot, Blush.pot, etc.).

  OR

- Click **Format**.

- Click **Apply Design**.

- Select a template design.

- Click **Apply**.

Template designs are applied to all the slides in a presentation.

- To change the template design, you may follow one of the following three procedures:

  - Double-click the template name on the Status bar.

  - Select Apply Design from the Format menu.

  - Click the Apply Design button  on the Standard toolbar.

  Once the Apply Design Template dialog box appears, you may select and apply another template.

- Sometimes, however, template color can be distracting while creating a presentation. To display the slide in black and white, click the Black and White View button on the Standard toolbar, or select Black and White from the View menu. If Slide Miniature is also selected in the View menu, a miniature of the slide appears in color.

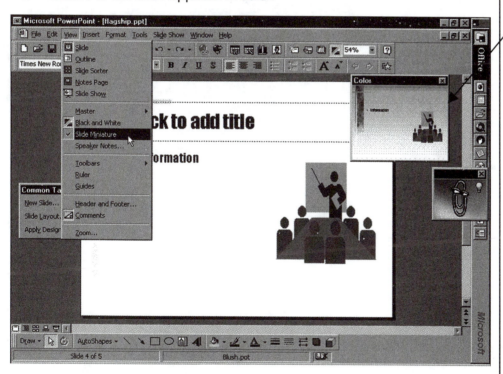

EXERCISE DIRECTIONS

PART I

1. Open ⌨**WPRT**, or open 💾**03WPRT**.
2. Display slide 2, Agenda.
3. Create a new slide using the Text & Clip AutoLayout.

    ✓ *This slide will be inserted after slide 2.*

4. Enter the title and bulleted information shown in Illustration A. Insert any relevant clip art.
5. Create another new slide, this time using the Clip Art & Text AutoLayout.

6. Enter the title and bulleted information shown in Illustration B. Insert any relevant clip art.
7. Switch to Slide Sorter view.
8. Switch back to Slide view.
9. In the Print dialog box, select Handouts with six slides per page as the Print what option.
10. Print one copy in black and white.
11. Close the file; save the changes.

ILLUSTRATION A

Programming Projections

- Programming Success
  - The Hollies
  - Moon Rock
  - Just Plain Folk

ILLUSTRATION B

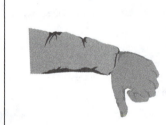

Programs Replaced

- The Quarter Mile
- The Toads
- Talk Radio

PART II

1. Open ⌨**MAGAZINE**, or open 💾**03MAGAZINE**.

2. Create a new slide using the Text & Clip AutoLayout.

   ✓ *This slide will be inserted after slide 1. You will move the slides into the desired order in the next exercise.*

3. Enter the title and bulleted information shown in Illustration C. Insert any relevant clip art.

4. Create another new slide; use the Clip Art & Text AutoLayout.

5. Enter the title and bulleted information shown in Illustration D. Insert any relevant clip art.

6. Switch to Slide Sorter view.

7. Switch back to Slide view.

8. Change the template to the **Angles** design.

9. Change the slide view to black and white. Display the slide miniature. Change the slide view back to color.

10. Use the default print slide setup.

11. In the Print dialog box, select Handouts with six slides per page as the Print <u>w</u>hat option.

12. Print one copy in black and white.

13. Close the file; save the changes.

ILLUSTRATION C

ILLUSTRATION D

KEYSTROKES

DISPLAY SLIDE VIEW

Click **Slide View** button .... 🔲

OR

1. Click **View** .... `Alt` + `V`

2. Click **Slide** .... `S`

CHANGE LAYOUT

SLIDE VIEW

1. Click **Slide Layout** button .... 🔳
on Standard toolbar.

   OR

   a. Click **Format** .... `Alt` + `O`

   b. Click **Slide Layout** .... `L`

2. Select a desired layout.

3. Click **Apply** .... `Alt` + `A`

   OR

   Click **Reapply** .... `Alt` + `A`

CHANGE TEMPLATE

1. Click **Apply Design** button .... 🔳
on Standard toolbar.

   OR

   Double-click template name on Status
   bar (Angles.pot, Blush.pot, etc.).

   OR

   a. Click **Format** .... `Alt` + `O`

   b. Click **Apply Design** .... `Y`

2. Select a template design.

3. Click **Apply** .... `Alt` + `P`

UNDO

Ctrl + Z

Click **Undo** button
on Standard toolbar .... ↰

OR

1. Click **Edit** .... `Alt` + `E`

2. Click **Undo** .... `U`

REDO

Ctrl + Y

Click **Redo** button
on Standard toolbar .... ↱▾

OR

1. Click **Edit** .... `Alt` + `E`

2. Click **Redo** .... `R`

USE SLIDE AUTOLAYOUT
TO INSERT CLIP ART

1. Select a an AutoLayout that has a clip
art option available.

2. Double-click clip art placeholder in
template.

   OR

   a. Click **Insert** .... `Alt` + `I`

   b. Click **Picture** .... `P`

   c. Click **Clip Art** .... `C`

3. Click desired clip art graphic.

4. Click **Insert** .... `Alt` + `I`

AUTOCLIPART

1. Click **Tools** .... `Alt` + `T`

2. Click **AutoClipArt** .... `U`

3. Click first list arrow to display words in
the presentation that have a relevant
picture.

4. Select word.

5. Click **View Clip Art** .... `Alt` + `V`

6. Select relevant picture.

7. Click **Insert** .... `Alt` + `I`

■ **Move, Copy, Duplicate, and Delete Slides**
■ **Slide Sorter View**

NOTES

Move, Copy, Duplicate, and Delete Slides

■ Each slide in a presentation is part of the entire presentation. Slides may be moved, copied, duplicated, or deleted within the presentation. You can also move and copy slides from one presentation to another.

■ The **Duplicate Slide** command lets you create a copy of a slide in Slide view. The Copy command is not available in Slide view. If you have created a custom slide that contains effects that you want to repeat on subsequent slides, you can duplicate the slide. You can also use the Duplicate Slide command in Outline and Slide Sorter views. To duplicate a slide, select the slide and then select <u>D</u>uplicate Slide from the <u>I</u>nsert menu.

Slide Sorter View

■ You can move, copy, or delete slides using menu commands or Cut/Copy and Paste procedures. It is easiest and most efficient to perform these tasks in Slide Sorter view since all of the slides are displayed in miniature and you can easily see the flow of the presentation in this view.

You should save a presentation before moving, copying, duplicating, or deleting slides to prevent loss of data. If you move, copy, or delete a slide then change your mind, use the Undo feature to reverse the action.

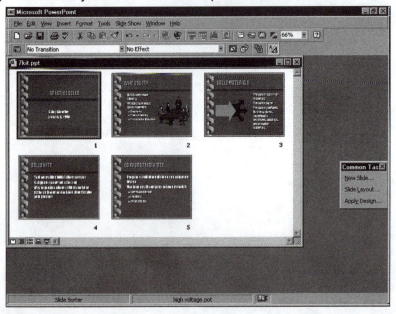

- To move, copy, or delete a slide in Slide Sorter view, click the Slide Sorter View button , or select Sli<u>d</u>e Sorter from the <u>V</u>iew menu.

- Select the slide to be moved, copied, or deleted. (Selected slides are outlined by a dark, double border.) You can select slides using any one of the following techniques:
  - Click the desired slide.
  - Press the insertion point arrow keys until a dark border outlines the desired slide.
  - Press Shift and click each slide when you want to select multiple slides. Selecting multiple slides allows you to move, copy, duplicate, or delete them as a group.

- The easiest way to move a slide in Slide Sorter view is to select it and drag it to a new location. When the slide is being moved, the mouse pointer becomes a slide icon and a vertical bar identifies the new position of the slide.

- When the bar appears in the position where you want to place the slide, release the mouse button.

- To copy a slide, press Ctrl and drag the slide you want to copy to a new location. The mouse pointer becomes a slide icon carrying a plus sign (+).

- To delete a slide, select it and press Delete.

Return to Slide View

- Since you cannot edit slide contents in Slide Sorter view, you will need to return to Slide view to make changes and adjust text. You can return to Slide view using one of the following techniques:
  - Double-click a slide.
  - Select the desired slide and click the Slide View button .
  - Select the desired slide, and select <u>S</u>lide from the <u>V</u>iew menu.

It is most efficient to move, copy, duplicate, or delete slides in Slide Sorter view because you are able to see all the slides in the presentation at once.

To return to Slide view from Slide Sorter view:
- Click **View**.
- Click **Slide**.

  OR

- Click the **Slide View** button.

EXERCISE DIRECTIONS

1. Open **WPRT**, or open **04WPRT**.
2. Create a new slide using the 2 Column Text AutoLayout.
3. Enter the text shown in Illustration A.
4. Create another new slide using the Clip Art & Text AutoLayout.
5. Enter the text shown in Illustration B. Insert a relevant graphic.
6. Switch to Slide Sorter view.
7. Move the Agenda slide after the title slide.
8. Move the Programming Projections slide to make it slide 4.
9. Check your presentation with the slides Shown in Illustration C.
10. Apply the **Contemporary Portrait** template design.
11. View your presentation in black and white.
12. Print one copy of the presentation as Handouts with six slides per page in pure black and white.
13. Close the file; save the changes.

ILLUSTRATION A

In the Works . . .

- Gossip Galore
  - Top gossip columnists tell all about Hollywood's brightest stars
- Feminine Focus
  - News magazine concerned with women's issues

ILLUSTRATION B

New Employees

- Jane Susans, Production Assistant
- Kenneth Coleman, Sound Specialist
- Jerry Gomez, Sports Announcer

DESIRED RESULTS

WPRT Television

**Management Team
Annual Meeting**

SLIDE 1

Agenda

▊ The Year in Review
▊ Programming Projections
▊ The Fall Forecast
▊ New Affiliates

SLIDE 2

In the Works . . .

▊ Gossip Galore
　▏ Top gossip columnists tell all about Hollywood's brightest stars

▊ Feminine Focus
　▏ News magazine concerned with women's issues

SLIDE 3

Programming Projections

▊ Programming Success
　▏ The Hollies
　▏ Moon Rock
　▏ Just Plain Folk

SLIDE 4

New Employees

▊ Jane Susans, Production Assistant
▊ Kenneth Coleman, Sound Specialist
▊ Jerry Gomez, Sports Announcer

SLIDE 5

Programs Replaced

▊ The Quarter Mile
▊ The Toads
▊ Talk Radio

SLIDE 6

The Year in Review

▊ Organizational Changes
▊ Sales Records
▊ Ratings Review

SLIDE 7

KEYSTROKES

MOVE SLIDES

SLIDE SORTER VIEW

1. Select slide to move.
2. Drag slide to new location.

COPY SLIDES

SLIDE SORTER VIEW

1. Select slide to copy.
2. Press **Ctrl** and drag slide to new location.

DUPLICATE SLIDES

SLIDE SORTER VIEW

1. Select slide to duplicate.
2. Click **Insert** .... Alt + I
3. Click **Duplicate Slide.** .... D

DELETE SLIDES

SLIDE SORTER VIEW

1. Select slide to delete.
2. Press **Delete** .... Del

Next Exercise

NOTES

Outline View

■ Outline view displays slide text as titles and subtitles in an outline format to give an overview of the contents of a presentation. This view is most often used to help organize a presentation.

■ Note the illustration below of the presentation displayed in Outline view. Slides are numbered down the left side of the screen and slide icons identify the start of each new slide. A miniature of the selected slide appears in the Color Window. If the miniature is not on screen, select Slide Miniature from the View menu.

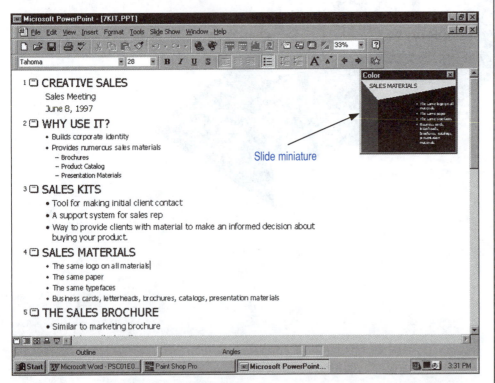

Slide miniature

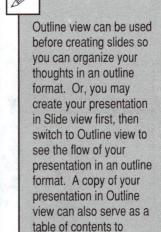

Outline view can be used before creating slides so you can organize your thoughts in an outline format. Or, you may create your presentation in Slide view first, then switch to Outline view to see the flow of your presentation in an outline format. A copy of your presentation in Outline view can also serve as a table of contents to distribute to your audience.

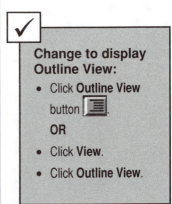

Change to display Outline View:

• Click **Outline View** button.
   OR
• Click **View**.
• Click **Outline View**.

■ If Slide Miniature is turned off, you will not see graphics and objects in Outline view. However, a slide that contains such items will be identified by shapes in the miniature slide icon that appears to the right of the slide number. For example, 5 indicates that there are graphics and text on slide 5.

- To switch to Outline view, click the Outline View button 🔲, or select Outline from the View menu.

- The Outlining toolbar replaces the Drawing toolbar in the presentation window. The Outlining toolbar contains tools for executing common outlining tasks more efficiently. Many of these tasks are not available on the menus.

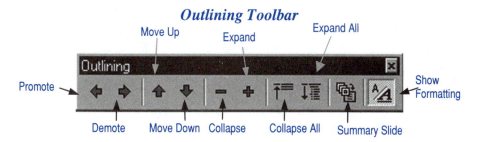

Outlining Toolbar

- **Promote/Demote** buttons 🔲 🔲 let you quickly move text up or down a level. For example, you can reformat bulleted text as title text (promote) and title text as item text (demote).

- **Move Up/Move Down** buttons 🔲 🔲 let you select text from one slide and move it to a new location, either up or down. These buttons do not affect the hierarchical level of the outline text, however; level two text remains level two text but physically moves up or down on the outline screen. This procedure can be used to move or rearrange individual text items or complete slides.

- **Collapse** button 🔲 lets you remove all levels of subitem text from the outline display for individual slides, or for multiple slides when they are selected as a group.

- **Expand** button 🔲 lets you display all levels of text for the selected slide(s).

- **Collapse All** button 🔲 lets you display only the title text for all slides in a presentation.

- **Expand All** button 🔲 lets you display all levels of text for every slide in the presentation.

- **Show Formatting** button 🔲 lets you display formatted and enhanced text as it appears on the slide. When this feature is inactive, text for all slides appears as plain text in the default font.

Add Slides in Outline View

- The same four procedures can be used to add slides in Outline view that were used to add slides in Slide view:

  - Click the New Slide button  on the Standard toolbar.
  - Click New Slide on Common Task toolbar.

Common Tas ☒
New Slide...
Slide Layout...
Apply Design...

  - Press Ctrl+M.
  - Select Insert, New Slide from the menu.

Print an Outline

- You can print an outline using the same basic procedures that were used to print copies of your slides. However, you must select Outline View from the Print what drop-down list.

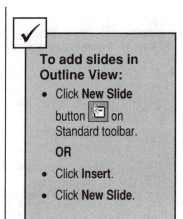

To add slides in Outline View:
- Click **New Slide** button on Standard toolbar.

  OR
- Click **Insert**.
- Click **New Slide**.

In this exercise, you will create a presentation in Outline view. After creating the presentation, you will move and add slides and print the presentation.

EXERCISE DIRECTIONS

√1. Create a New blank Presentation. Click Cancel to exit the New Slide dialog box.

√2. Switch to Outline view.

√3. Enter the following titles and subtitles to create your outline:

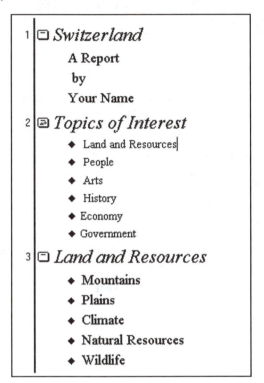

Hint: To move down to a lower level of bullets, click on the Demote button on the Outlining toolbar, or press Tab before typing. To move up a level, click the Promote button, or press Shift+Tab.

4. Switch to Slide view.

5. Display Slide 1. Reapply the Title slide AutoLayout.

6. Display Slide 2. Change the Slide AutoLayout to Clip Art & Text. Insert a relevant graphic.

7. Change the presentation template to **High Voltage**.

√8. Return to Outline view and insert a new slide after slide 3 that reads:

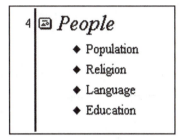

9. Switch to Slide view.

10. Change the layout of slide 4 to Text & Clip Art. Insert a relevant graphic.

√11. Spell check.

√12. In the Page Setup dialog box, change the orientation for Notes, handouts & outline to Landscape.

√13. Print one copy as handouts (6 slides per page) in black and white.

14. Save the file; name it **SWITZERLAND**. Fill in the appropriate summary information.

√15. Close the file; save the changes.

KEYSTROKES

SWITCH TO OUTLINE VIEW

Click **Outline View** button.............. ▣

OR

1. Click **V**iew .... Alt + V

2. Click **O**utline View...................... O

ADD SLIDES IN OUTLINE VIEW

Ctrl + M

Click **New Slide** button .... ▣
on Standard toolbar.

OR

1. Click **I**nsert .... Alt + I

2. Click **N**ew Slide .... N

ADD TEXT IN OUTLINE VIEW

Click ◆ to indent.............................. Tab

or add subitems.

✓ *To add a bulleted item under the title line, press Enter and then press Tab.*

OR

Click ◆ to go back................. Shift + Tab
one text or subitem level.

Exercise

6

■ **Summary**

In this exercise, you will create a presentation in Outline view. You will move the slides, change the layouts of selected slides, and print the presentation.

EXERCISE DIRECTIONS

1. Create a new, blank presentation. Click Cancel in the New Slide dialog box.

2. Switch to Outline view.

3. Create the outline shown in Illustration A.

4. Print one copy of the outline.

5. Switch to Slide view.

6. Change the presentation template to Contemporary.

7. Switch to Slide Sorter view.

8. Delete slide 5 (Memorable Moments).

9. Undo the deletion.

10. Display slide 5 (Memorable Moments) and change the AutoLayout to Clip Art & Text. Insert any relevant graphic.

11. Display slide 6 (Looking Ahead) and change the AutoLayout to Text & Clip Art. Insert any relevant graphic.

12. Spell check.

13. Switch to Slide Sorter view.

14. Print the presentation as handouts (6 slides per page) in black and white.

15. Save the file; name it **OLYMPIC**. Fill in the appropriate summary information.

16. Close the presentation window.

ILLUSTRATION A

1 ☐ The Olympic Games
   An Historic Perspective

2 ☐ First Modern Games
   ▪ Athens, 1896
   ▪ 14 nations
   ▪ 285 athletes
   ▪ 42 events in nine sports

3 ☐ Politics and the Olympics
   • Berlin, 1936--Hitler's impact on the games
   • Mexico City, 1968--Social and political riots in lead-up to Olympics
   • Munich, 1972--Terrorist attack on 11 Israeli athletes
   • Montreal, 1976--Racial tensions
   • Moscow, 1980--U.S. boycott
   • Los Angeles, 1984--U.S.S.R. boycott

4 ☐ Centennial Games
   ▪ Atlanta, 1996
   ▪ 197 nations
   ▪ 11,000 athletes
   ▪ 250 events in 56 sports

5 ☐ Memorable Moments
   • Nadia Comaneci scores a perfect 10
   • Muhammad Ali lights Olympic flame
   • U.S. women's soccer team wins first gold medal in the sport

6 ☐ Looking Ahead
   • Sydney, Australia
   • Year 2000

ILLUSTRATION B

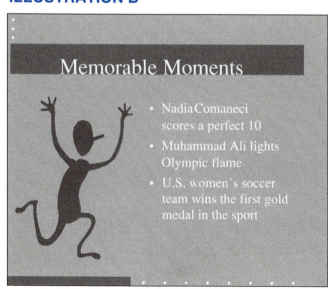

ILLUSTRATION C

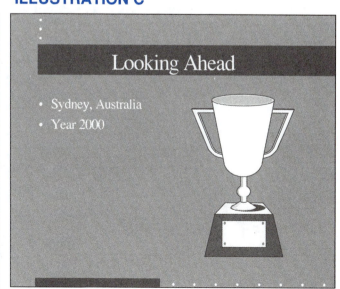

Exercise 7

■ **Summary**

In this exercise, you will create an informative presentation based on a report.

EXERCISE DIRECTIONS

1. Review the report in the illustration on the following page.

2. Using the information contained in the report, develop a presentation about hieroglyphics and how they were used by the Ancient Egyptians. Include each of the following elements:
   a. a template
   b. a title slide
   c. at least two bulleted list slides
   d. at least one two-Column text slide
   e. at least two slides including clip art

3. Check your presentation through all views, reorganizing, adding, and deleting slides where necessary.

4. Spell check.

5. Save the presentation; name it **EGYPT**.

6. Print the presentation as a handout (6 slides per page) in black and white.

7. Print a copy of the presentation as an outline.

8. Close the presentation window.

Hieroglyphics of the Ancient Egyptians

INTRODUCTION

Ancient Egyptian hieroglyphics, one of the world's first written languages, are composed of pictorial images called phonograms (sound signs) and ideograms (picture signs). The word *hieroglyphic* is derived from the Greek word *hieros*, meaning sacred, and *gluphe*, meaning carving. This Egyptian script was used primarily for engraving epithets, titles, bureaucratic records, religious texts, and other important documents.

IDEOGRAMS AND PHONOGRAMS

Hieroglyphic writing is made up of two basic components: ideograms and phonograms. Ideograms are images that represent a specific object or idea.   A picture of a sun, for example, can mean "sun" or "day." Phonograms are drawings that convey a phonetic sound, such as a consonant or combination of consonants. Some images can serve as both ideograms and phonograms, depending on the context. Most hieroglyphic texts are a combination of sound signs and word signs, in which the phonograms often determine a specific meaning for the ideograms. The ideogram for "house," for example, followed by the phonogram of walking legs, suggests the meaning "to go out."

INFLUENCE ON OUR ALPHABET

Hieroglyphic writing clearly influenced the development of modern alphabets, including the one we use today. The capital letter "A" likely came from the Egyptian hieroglyph of an eagle, and the lowercase "a" originated from the hieroglyph of an oxhead.

DECIPHERING HIEROGLYPHICS

Egyptian hieroglyphics date as far back as 3100 BC and were used as a written language system for approximately 3,500 years. In the earliest years of Egyptian civilization, there were about 700 hieroglyphs, and by the time the system became obsolete, the number of hieroglyphs increased to several thousand. As writing evolved, the Egyptians developed a more efficient cursive script that could be written with ink on papyrus paper, thus eliminating the need for hieroglyphics.

HOW HIEROGLYPHICS WORKED

Hieroglyphics could be written both horizontally or vertically, usually from right to left. The symbols included nouns, verbs, prepositions, and other common parts of speech following strict grammatical rules of order. For hundreds of years, the structure and meaning of the hieroglyphics remained a mystery. The Romans believed the images were symbolic, not phonetic, a theory which lasted through the Renaissance. It was not until 1799, when a soldier in Napoleon's army discovered the famous Rosetta stone that the true meaning of hieroglyphic symbols would become known.

THE ROSETTA STONE

In 196 BC, during the reign of King Ptolemy V Epipanes, temple priests engraved a decree praising the events of his kingship on a black basalt slab, now known as the Rosetta stone. It became the key to unlocking the code of Egyptian hieroglyphics because the same text was also inscribed in demotic Egyptian and ancient Greek. Demotic script was a later, more common form of hieroglyphics used in everyday documents. Although Napoleon's troops uncovered the stone during his campaign in Egypt in 1799, scholars did not set to work deciphering the text until 1821. British physicist and physician Thomas Young determined the direction in which the symbols should be read, and French Egyptologist and linguist Jean-Claude Champollion recognized hieroglyphics as phonetic. They completed the decipherment in 1822, enabling scholars to understand all forms of Egyptian hieroglyphics.

Next
Lesson

Lesson 2

Enhance Slides; Work with Text and Objects
Exercises 8-13

- Select, Align, and Change the Appearance of Text
- Change a Slide's Color Scheme
- Change Slide Background
- Change Case
- Copy Text Formatting
- Move and Copy Text
- Increase/Decrease Paragraph Spacing
- Move and Size Placeholders
- Use Slide and Title Master
- Insert Slide Numbers, Date and Time, and Footer Text
- Save as Template
- Format Bullets
- Draw Graphic Objects
- Use AutoShapes
- Create Text Objects
- Group and Ungroup Objects
- Layer Objects
- Floating Toolbars

Exercise 8

- **Select Text** ■ **Align Text** ■ **Replace Fonts**
- **Change the Appearance of Text** ■ **Change Case**
- **Change a Slide's Color Scheme** ■ **Change Slide Background**

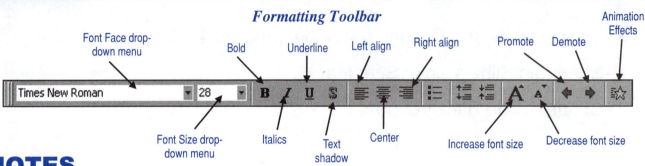

Formatting Toolbar

Font Face drop-down menu · Bold · Underline · Left align · Right align · Promote · Demote · Animation Effects

Font Size drop-down menu · Italics · Text shadow · Center · Increase font size · Decrease font size

NOTES

Select Text

- When you point to text with the mouse, the mouse pointer changes to an I-beam to signify that the text insertion mode is active. Click the text you want to edit, and use the following techniques for selecting blocks of text in PowerPoint:

  - Double-click to select a word.
  - Triple-click to select a paragraph, complete title, or bulleted item, including all subitems.
  - Click and drag across text to highlight it.

Align Text

- PowerPoint lets you align text to the left, center, or right in a placeholder or text box. Because the most frequently used alignments in PowerPoint are left, right, and center, buttons for these three alignment options are included on the Formatting toolbar. Justified alignment is available by selecting Alignment, Justify from the Format menu.

- To change the alignment of title text or text for one bulleted item, position the I-beam in the title or bulleted item and click the desired alignment button.

- To change the alignment for more than one bulleted item, select text you want to change before clicking the alignment button or selecting the alignment option from the Format menu.

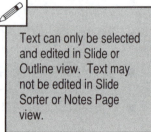

Text can only be selected and edited in Slide or Outline view. Text may not be edited in Slide Sorter or Notes Page view.

While you can set alignment in both Outline and Slide views, use Slide view to change text alignment because text formatting is displayed in this view.

■ While you can set alignment in either Outline or Slide view, it is better to do so in Slide view, because text formatting is displayed in this view.

■ When you want to change the alignment of title text, all text in the title placeholder for that slide is realigned. To align text on one line of a title differently from text of other lines, remove the lines you want to align differently from the title placeholder and include them in the body placeholder. Each line in the body placeholder can then be aligned separately.

Change the Appearance of Text

■ PowerPoint controls the font face, size, emphasis (bold, italics, shadow, underline), and color of text on each slide layout. However, you can change the font face and other attributes of any text on a PowerPoint slide at any time.

■ Format changes and enhancements affect the word in which the insertion point rests unless you have selected specific text.

■ Use the Formatting toolbar to change one text attribute quickly; use the Font dialog box to apply more than one change, or to apply a different font color. See the Keystrokes on page 58 for procedures for applying specific text changes.

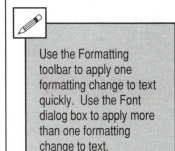

Use the Formatting toolbar to apply one formatting change to text quickly. Use the Font dialog box to apply more than one formatting change to text.

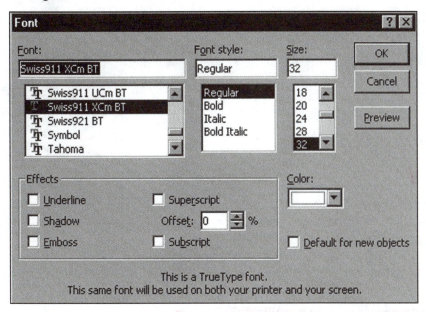

■ The Formatting toolbar contains buttons to change the appearance of text:

• Use the Bold **B**, Italics **I**, or Underline **U** buttons to apply these attributes.

• Use the **Increase/Decrease Font Size** buttons **A A** to increase or decrease the font size incrementally.

• Use the **Text Shadow** button **S** to apply shadow effects to text.

• Use the **Promote (Indent less)** and **Demote (Indent more)** buttons ← → to adjust the levels of bulleted items.

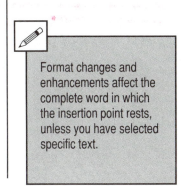

Format changes and enhancements affect the complete word in which the insertion point rests, unless you have selected specific text.

- Use the **Animation Effects** button to apply animation to objects or text. Animation will activate in Slide Show view. (*Animation effects will be covered in Exercise 15.*)
- Use the **Font Size** drop-down menu `24` to apply a different font size.
- Use the **Font Face** drop-down menu `Times New Roman` to apply a different font face.

■ The Show Formatting button , available on the Outlining toolbar in Outline view and on the Slide Sorter toolbar in Slide Sorter view, is defaulted to display font style, font size, bold, italics, and underline. When you turn off the Show Formatting feature, text appears in the default font with no enhancements.

Change Case

■ The change case feature lets you change an existing block of text to sentence case, lowercase, uppercase, title case, or toggle case. To change case, highlight the text and select Change Ca<u>s</u>e from the F<u>o</u>rmat menu. In the Change Case dialog box that follows, choose the desired case.

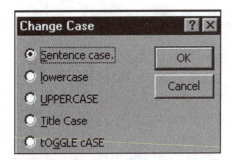

Change Slide Color Scheme

■ Each template design has a predefined color scheme. Specific colors were chosen for the slide background, title text, fills, lines, shadows, and accents. PowerPoint lets you change the entire color scheme of your presentation or change individual parts (for example, line colors and slide background only). You may change the color scheme of one or all slides in your presentation.

■ To change a slide's color scheme, select Slide <u>C</u>olor Scheme from the F<u>o</u>rmat menu or right-click the slide and select Slide <u>C</u>olor Scheme from the shortcut menu. In the Color Scheme dialog box that follows, you may select one of the predefined options indicated on the Standard tab.

There are three types of font faces: serif, sans serif, and script. A serif font has lines curves, or edges extending from the ends of the letter (**T**), a sans serif font is straight-edged (**T**), and a script font imitates handwriting (𝒯).

Text must be selected before you can use the Change Case command.

To change case:
- Select text.
- Click **Format**.
- Click **Change Case**.
- Choose desired case option from the Change Case dialog box.

Standard
tab

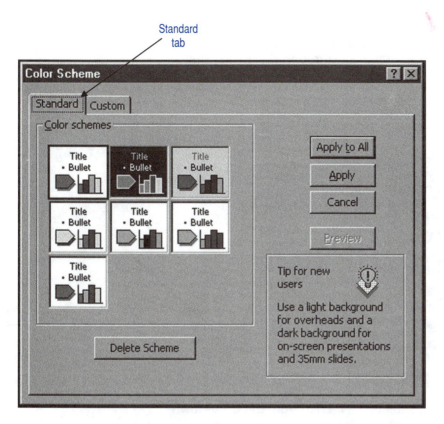

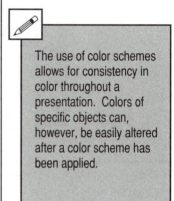

The use of color schemes allows for consistency in color throughout a presentation. Colors of specific objects can, however, be easily altered after a color scheme has been applied.

■ To make custom changes to individual slide parts, click the Custom tab. Select the item to change (Background, Text and Lines, Title Text, etc.) from the Scheme colors list. Then click the Change Color button to select from a palette of additional colors. The preview window displays the results of your choices. Click Apply to All to change all slides or click Apply to change only the current slide.

Custom tab

Select item
to change.

Preview
window

Click to
display
palette of
additional
colors.

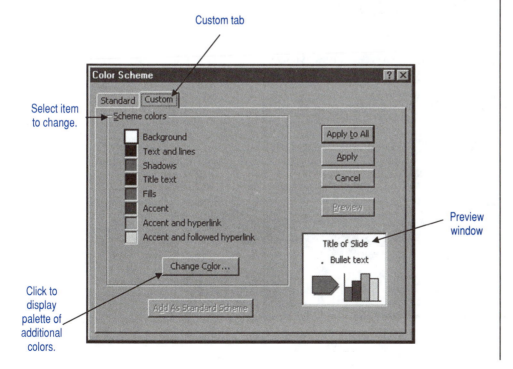

Change Slide Background

- To change a slide's background, color, shadows, pattern or texture, select Background from the Format menu. In the Background dialog box that follows, click the list arrow.

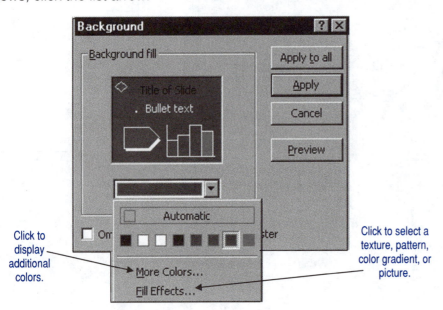

Click to display additional colors.

Click to select a texture, pattern, color gradient, or picture.

- To change the background color, select a new color from the drop-down palette. Or click More Colors from the drop-down list to select from additional background color options.

- To apply a color gradient, texture, pattern, or picture to the slide background, click Fill Effects from the drop-down list. In the Fill Effects dialog box that follows, click the appropriate tab and select the desired options. A preview window displays the result of your selection.

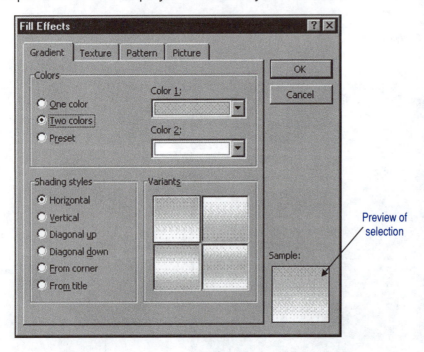

Preview of selection

Replace Fonts

- You may replace one font face with another font face on all slides at once by selecting **Replace Fonts** from the F**o**rmat menu. In the Replace Font dialog box which follows, select a font on the slides to replace in the Replace text box, select a font to replace it with in the **W**ith text box, then click **R**eplace.

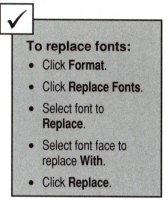

To replace fonts:
- Click **Format**.
- Click **Replace Fonts**.
- Select font to **Replace**.
- Select font face to replace **With**.
- Click **Replace**.

- The Show Formatting button on the Outlining toolbar is defaulted to display font style, font size, bold, italics, and underline. When you turn off the Show Formatting feature, text appears in the default font with no enhancements. The Show Formatting icon is available in Outline and Slide Sorter views.

In this exercise, you will manipulate placeholders and change the size and color of text on slides.

EXERCISE DIRECTIONS

1. Open WPRT, or open 08WPRT.

2. Using Slide view, replace the font faces on all slides with Arial.

3. Center align the titles in slides 2-6.

4. Increase the font size of the bulleted text on slide 4, Programming Projections, using the Increase Font Size button on the Formatting toolbar.

5. Italicize subtitles on slide 1.

6. Switch to Outline view.

7. Use the Show Formatting button on the Outlining toolbar to turn the formatting on and off.

8. Switch back to Slide view.

9. Insert a new slide after slide 6 that reads:

WPRT Syndicated Shows
• The Morning Commute
• Rock Block
• Street Beat
• Sounds of Jazz

10. Center the title.

11. Switch to Slide Sorter view.

12. Print one copy as handouts with six slides per page in black and white.

13. Close the file; save the changes.

WPRT Television

Management Team
Annual Meeting

SLIDE 1

Agenda

▌ The Year in Review
▌ Programming Projections
▌ The Fall Forecast
▌ New Affiliates

SLIDE 2

In the Works . . .

▌ Gossip Galore
  ▌ Top gossip columnists tell all about Hollywood's brightest stars

▌ Feminine Focus
  ▌ New magazine concerned with women's issues

SLIDE 3

Programming Projections

▌ Programming Success
  ▌ The Hollies
  ▌ Moon Rock
  ▌ Just Plain Folk

SLIDE 4

Continued…

New Employees

- Jane Susans, Production Assistant
- Kenneth Coleman, Sound Specialist
- Jerry Gomez, Sports Announcer

SLIDE 5

Programs Replaced

- The Quarter Mile
- The Toads
- Talk Radio

SLIDE 6

WPRT Syndicated Shows

- The Morning Commute
- Rock Block
- Street Beat
- Sounds of Jazz

SLIDE 7

The Year in Review

- Organizational Changes
- Sales Records
- Ratings Review

SLIDE 8

KEYSTROKES

ALIGN TEXT

1. Position insertion point in text to align.
   OR
   Select text to align.
2. Click desired Alignment button on Formatting toolbar:
   - Click **Left**................................. ▤
   - Click **Right**.............................. ▤
   - Click **Center**........................... ▤
   OR
   a. Click **Format**..................... `Alt`+`O`
   b. Click **Alignment**...................... `A`
   c. Select desired alignment:
      - **Left**................................. `L`
      - **Center**............................. `C`
      - **Right**.............................. `R`
      - **Justify**............................ `J`

CHANGE FONT FACE

   ✓ *The following procedures can only be performed in Slide view.*

1. Position insertion point in word to format.
   OR
   Select text to format.
2. Select......... | Times New Roman ▾ |
   desired font from Formatting toolbar
   Font Face drop-down menu.
   OR
   a. Click **Format**..................... `Alt`+`O`
   b. Click **Font** .... `F`
   c. Click the **Font** box............. `Alt`+`F`
      and select desired font face.
   d. Click **OK**................................ `Enter`

CHANGE FONT SIZE

1. Position insertion point in word to format.
   OR
   Select text to change.
2. Select desired size .... | 24 ▾ |
   from Formatting toolbar
   Font Size drop-down menu.
   OR
   1. Click **Format**..................... `Alt`+`O`
   2. Click **Font** .... `F`
   3. Click the **Size** box............... `Alt`+`S`
      and select desired font size.
   4. Click **OK** .... `Enter`
   OR
   Click `A⁺ A⁻` on the Formatting toolbar to increase/decrease font size incrementally.

CHANGE EMPHASIS (BOLD, ITALICS, SHADOW, UNDERLINE, COLOR)

1. Position insertion point in word to change.
   OR
   Select text to change.
2. Click desired emphasis button on Formatting toolbar:
   - **Bold**................................ `B`
   - **Italic**............................... `I`
   - **Underline** .... `U`
   OR
   a. Click **Format**..................... `Alt`+`O`
   b. Click **Font** .... `F`
   c. Click **Font Style**............. `Alt`+`O`
   d. Select desired options.
   e. Select desired emphasis style(s) from the Effects section of the dialog box:
      - **Underline** .... `Alt`+`U`
      - **Shadow** .... `Alt`+`A`
      - **Emboss** .... `Alt`+`E`
      - **Superscript** .... `Alt`+`R`
      - **Subscript** .... `Alt`+`B`
   f. Click **Color**..................... `Alt`+`C`
      drop-down list box and select a new font color, if desired.
   g. Click **OK**............................. `Enter`

CHANGE CASE

1. Select text to change.
2. Click **Format**..................... `Alt`+`O`
3. Click **Change Case**....................... `E`
4. Select desired case:
   - **Sentence case**........................ `S`
   - **lowercase** .... `L`
   - **UPPERCASE** .... `U`
   - **Title Case**........................... `T`
   - **tOGGLE cASE** .... `G`

CHANGE SLIDE COLOR SCHEME

1. Click **F**ormat .... `Alt` + `O`
2. Click **Slide Color Scheme** .... `C`
3. Click Standard tab and select desired color schemes.
   OR
   a. Click **Custom** tab.
   b. Click item to change (Background, Text and Lines, etc.)
   c. Click **Change Color** .... `Alt` + `O`
   d. Select desired color.
   e. Click **OK** .... `Enter`
   f. Repeat for other items to change.
4. Click **Apply to All** .... `Alt` + `T`
   OR
   Click **Apply** .... `Alt` + `A`
   to apply changes to current slide only.

CHANGE SLIDE BACKGROUND

1. Click **F**ormat .... `Alt` + `O`
2. Click **Background** .... `K`
3. Click the **Background fill** .... `Alt` + `B`
   drop-down arrow.
4. Select a new background fill color from the drop-down list.
   OR
   a. Select **More Colors** .... `M`
      from the drop-down list.
   b. Click the **Standard** or **Custom** tab and select a different fill color from the additional options.
   OR
   a. Select **Fill Effects** .... `F`
      from the drop-down list.
   b. Select desired options from appropriate tabs.
   c. Click **OK** .... `Enter`
5. Click **Apply to all** .... `Alt` + `T`
   to apply background settings to the entire presentation.
   OR
   Click **Apply** .... `Alt` + `A`
   to apply the background setting to only the selected slide(s).

REPLACE FONT FACES

1. Click **F**ormat .... `Alt` + `O`
2. Click **Replace Fonts** .... `R`
3. Select font to **Replace** .... `Alt` + `P`
4. Select font face .... `Alt` + `W`
   to replace **With**.
5. Click **Replace** .... `Alt` + `R`

- Copy Text Formatting (Format Painter)
- Copy and Move Text on a Slide
- Increase/Decrease Paragraph Formatting
- Move and Size Placeholders

Format Painter

Increase Paragraph Spacing

Decrease Paragraph Spacing

NOTES

Copy Text Formatting (Format Painter)

- The Format Painter feature may be used in PowerPoint to copy formatting, such as font face, style, size, and color, from one part of text to another.

- To copy formatting from one location to another, select the text that contains the format you wish to copy. Then, click the Format Painter button on the Standard toolbar (the I-beam displays a paintbrush) and select the text to receive the format.

- To copy formatting from one location to several locations, select the text that contains the format you wish to copy, then double-click the Format Painter button . Select the text to receive the format, release the mouse button, and select additional text anywhere in the document.

- To turn off this feature and return the mouse pointer to an I-beam, click the Format Painter button again or press Escape.

- When you use the Format Painter in Outline view, some formatting will not appear until you return to Slide view.

Move and Copy Text on a Slide

- You can move text only in Slide or Outline views. However, it is more efficient to use Outline view to move or copy text from one slide to another.

- To select bulleted items to move or copy in Outline view, position the mouse pointer on the bullet until it turns to a four-headed arrow and click once. The bulleted item, as well as all its subitems, will be highlighted. To select text to move in Slide view, click and drag across it to highlight it.

- To move or copy text in Slide or Outline view, select the text, then select Cut or Copy and then Paste from the Edit menu; click the Cut, Copy or Paste buttons on the Formatting toolbar; or select and drag and drop the text. In addition, you may position the pointer in the text and then use the Move Up or Move Down buttons on the Outlining toolbar to reposition text up or down one line at a time in Outline view.

If you want to copy formatting to several different places in the text, highlight the text whose formatting you want to copy and double-click the Format Painter button. You can then select several separate lines or blocks of text. Click the format Painter button again when you are done.

You can move text only in Slide or Outline view. However, it is more efficient to use Outline view to move or copy text from one slide to another.

- You can also cut, copy and paste text by selecting the text, then right-clicking the mouse. The shortcut menu will appear, from which you can select the option you wish to perform.

- To move selected text using drag and drop, place the mouse pointer in the selection and drag it until you see a horizontal or vertical line positioned where you want to insert the text. Release the mouse button, and your text will drop into place. To copy selected text, press the Ctrl key while you drag and drop text.

    ✓ *Note: You can only copy text using drag and drop in Slide view. It does not work in Outline view.*

- Use cut/copy and paste techniques to copy text to more than one new location or to copy text to a different presentation. Use the drag-and-drop technique in Outline view to move or copy text to a different slide or to rearrange bulleted items. Use the drag-and-drop feature in Slide view to move text on one slide.

Increase/Decrease Paragraph Spacing

- The space between paragraphs may be adjusted incrementally by selecting the paragraphs to be affected and clicking the Increase or Decrease Paragraph Spacing button on the Formatting toolbar.

- You may also adjust paragraph spacing by a specific amount by selecting Line Spacing from the Format menu. In the Line Spacing dialog box that follows, click in the Before paragraph and After paragraph increment boxes and type in desired number of lines or points to place before and after each paragraph. Then click the drop-down list arrow and select a unit of measurement: points or lines.

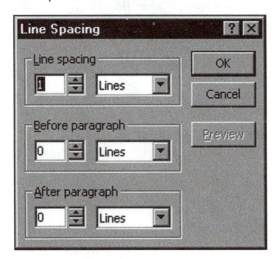

Move and Size Placeholders

- Text, clip art, and object placeholders can be moved, copied, sized, and deleted.

- To move, copy, size, or delete a placeholder, you must first display handles to put the placeholder into an edit mode. Click on the text to display the placeholder, then click on the placeholder border to display the handles. Click on the clip art or object to display the handles.

✓

To adjust line spacing by a specific amount:
- Select text to format.
- Click **Format**.
- Click **Line Spacing**.
- Enter desired amounts in Line Spacing dialog box.
- Click **OK**.

🖉

Paragraph spacing can be changed only in Slide view.

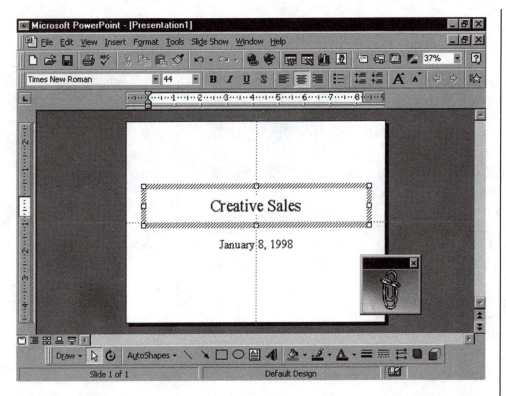

- When handles appear, you can **size** the placeholder: drag a top or bottom middle handle to change the vertical size (height); drag a left or right middle handle to change the horizontal size (width); drag a corner handle to size the placeholder proportionally. When you size a text placeholder, the text within it will adjust to the new borders.

- You can **move** the placeholder and its contents by displaying the handles, then placing the pointer on the border of the placeholder (not a handle). Click and hold the left mouse button while dragging the placeholder to the desired location.

In this exercise, you will manipulate placeholders and change the size and color of text on slides.

EXERCISE DIRECTIONS

1. Open ⌨**SWITZERLAND**, or open 💾**09SWIT**.
2. Switch to Slide view.
3. Replace the font with Arial.
4. Center the title slide on 2. Using Format Painter, apply centering to slides 3 and 4.
5. Display slide 1.
6. Center the subtitle text.
7. Move the placeholder to the lower-left corner.
8. Display the slide 2, Topics of Interest, and increase paragraph spacing.
9. Add a new slide at the end of the presentation using the Text & Clip Art AutoLayout.
10. Enter the following text:

> Culture
> - Literature
> - Art
> - Music
> - Libraries and Museums

11. Insert an appropriate graphic.
12. Change the AutoLayout of slide 3, Land and Resources, to Clip Art & Text.
13. Insert an appropriate graphic.
14. Switch to Outline view.
15. Add three slides to the end of the presentation.
16. Enter the following information for the first new slide:

> Economy
> - Agriculture
> - Forestry and Fishing
> - Mining
> - Manufacturing
> - Energy

17. Enter the following information for the second new slide:

> Government
> - Executive Power
> - Legislature
> - Judiciary

18. Enter the following information for the third and final new slide:

> History
> - Middle Ages
> - Struggle for Independence
> - Reformation
> - Unification

19. Switch to Slide view.
20. Change AutoLayout of slide 7, Government, to two-column text. Add the following text to the second column:

> - Currency and Banking
> - Foreign Trade

21. Add the following bulleted items to slide 8, History:

> - Neutrality
> - Domestic Issues

22. Apply the 2 Column Text AutoFormat to slide 8. Cut and paste the bullets so there are an equal number of bullets in each column.
23. Switch to slide 1. Increase the title font size to 54 point. Use the Format Painter to increase all the titles to 54 point. Adjust placeholders, if necessary, to keep the titles on one line.
24. Switch to Slide Sorter view. Display the slides in black and white.
25. Print one copy as handouts with six slides per page in black and white.
26. Close the file; save the changes.

SLIDE 1

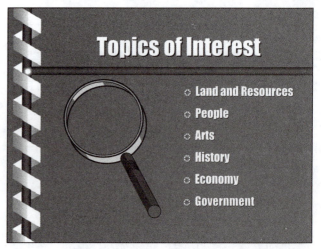

SLIDE 2

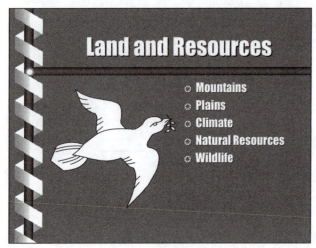

SLIDE 3

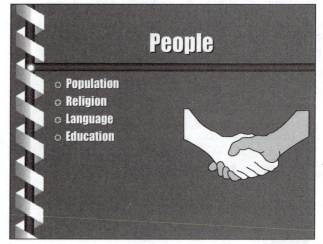

SLIDE 4

Continued…

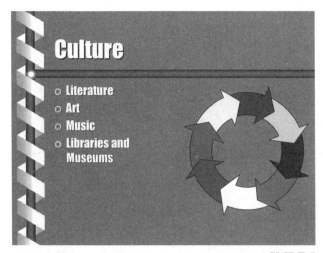

SLIDE 5

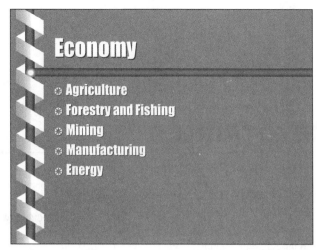

SLIDE 6

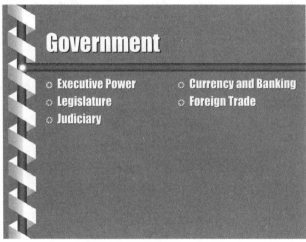

SLIDE 7

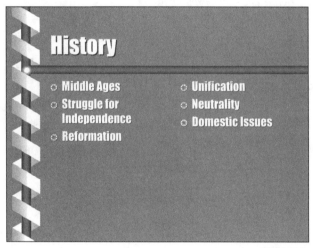

SLIDE 8

KEYSTROKES

COPY TEXT FORMATTING

1. Position insertion point in text containing formatting to copy.

2. Click the **Format Painter** button .... 🖌️ on the Standard toolbar.

   ✓ *Double-click the button if formatting is to be applied to multiple selections of text.*

3. Select text that you want to change or click to apply format to a word.

4. Press **Esc** to drop the .... [Esc] paintbrush, if necessary.

COPY

Ctrl + C

1. Select the text to copy.

2. Click the **Copy** button..................... 📋 on the Standard toolbar.

   OR

   • Click **Edit**........................ [Alt]+[E]

   • Click **Copy**............................... [C]

   OR

   Right-click and select **Copy**........... [C] from the Shortcut menu.

MOVE (CUT)

Ctrl + X

1. Select the text to move (cut).

2. Click the **Cut** button........................ ✂️ on the Standard toolbar.

   OR

   • Click **Edit**........................ [Alt]+[E]

   • Click **Cut**................................. [T]

   OR

   Right-click and select **Cut**.............. [T] from the shortcut menu.

PASTE

Ctrl + V

1. Position cursor where text is to be inserted.

2. Click the **Paste** button................... 📋 on the Standard toolbar.

   OR

   • Click **Edit**........................ [Alt]+[E]

   • Click **Paste**............................. [P]

   OR

   Right-click and select **Paste**........... [P] from the shortcut menu.

DRAG AND DROP

1. Select text to copy or move.

2. Position mouse pointer on selected text.

   ✓ *Mouse pointer must be a white pointer arrow ⇖ and box.*

3. Click and drag text until vertical bar (or horizontal bar, if in Outline view) appears in desired new text position.

   ✓ *To copy text using this process, hold down Ctrl ⇖ while dragging the text. You can only copy using this method in Slide view.*

4. Release mouse button.

INCREASE/DECREASE PARAGRAPH SPACING

1. Select paragraphs to be affected.

2. Click **Increase** or **Decrease** buttons on the Formatting toolbar to incrementally adjust spacing.

   OR

   a. Click **Format**.................... [Alt]+[O]

   b. Click **Line Spacing** .... [S]

   c. Enter the desired amount in **Before** .... [Alt]+[B], *number* **paragraph** text box.

      and/or

      Enter the desired amount in **After**.............. [Alt]+[A], *number* **paragraph** text box.

   d. Click **OK**................................ [Enter]

Next
Exercise

■ **Use Slide and Title Master**   ■ **Save As Template**
■ **Insert Slide Numbers, Date and Time, and Footer Text**
■ **Format Bullets**

NOTES

Use Slide and Title Master

■ The **Slide Master** contains the default settings for all the slides in a presentation, except the Title slide. The **Title Master** contains the default settings for the format of the Title slide.

■ By changing the content or formatting (font style, font size, color, position, tabs, indents, background, color scheme, template, etc.) of text or object placeholders on Slide Masters, all slides are automatically reformatted uniformly throughout the presentation. If, for example, you wanted to include clip art as your company's logo or a saying or quote on all slides in your presentation, you would include it on the Slide Master, and it would appear on all slides of your presentation.

If you change the formatting (font style, size, or color) of text or placeholders on the Slide Master, all other slides are automatically reformatted to match the master slide. However, not all slides have to follow the Slide Master. For example, one slide may use a different background. To do this, select the slide to receive the new background and click Apply, not Apply to All, in the background dialog box.

Slide Master

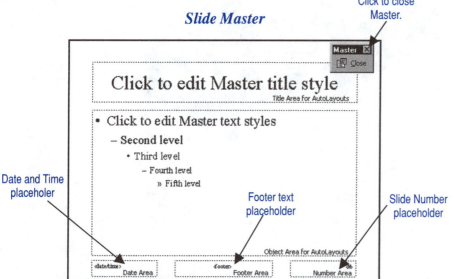

■ Changes made on the Slide Master affect *all* slides in a presentation *except* those using the Title slide AutoLayout. Changes to the Slide Master affect only the active presentation.

■ Formatting changes made to individual slides after the Slide Master has been created override changes made on the Slide Master.

■ Slide Master may be accessed by selecting Master from the View menu, and then selecting Slide Master. Or, you can hold down the Shift key as you click the Slide View button.

- After making the desired changes on the Slide Master, click the Slide View button and display each slide in the presentation to see the effects. You may need to make adjustments to the Slide Master after seeing the results on individual slides.

- If you do not want to include Slide Master objects on a particular slide, display that slide and select Background from the Format menu. In the Background dialog box that follows, select the Omit background graphics from the Master check box and click Apply.

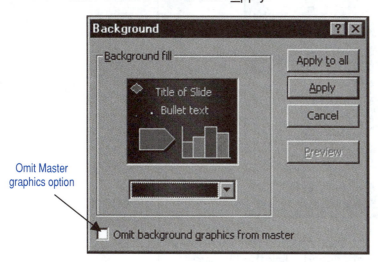

Omit Master
graphics option

Save As Template

- The changes made to a presentation or to Masters can be saved as a new template. The template can then be used to create new presentations, or can be applied to other existing presentations.

- To save your presentation as a template, select Save As from the File menu and then select Presentation Template from the Save as type drop-down list. Type a template name in the File name text box and select the drive and template folder where you want to store the template.

Insert Slide Numbers, Date and Time, and Footer Text

- Slide numbers, the date and/or time, and other text that you designate may be included in the footer area on an individual slide or on all slides. To do so, select Header and Footer from the View menu. In the Header and Footer dialog box that follows, click the appropriate check box to indicate whether you wish the Date and time, Slide number or Footer text to be on the current slide (Apply) or on all slides (Apply to All).

To save a presentation as a template:

- Click **File**.

- Click **Save As**.

- Select Presentation Templates from the Save as type drop-down list.

- Enter a name for the template.

- Select folder where you wish to save template.

- Click **Save**.

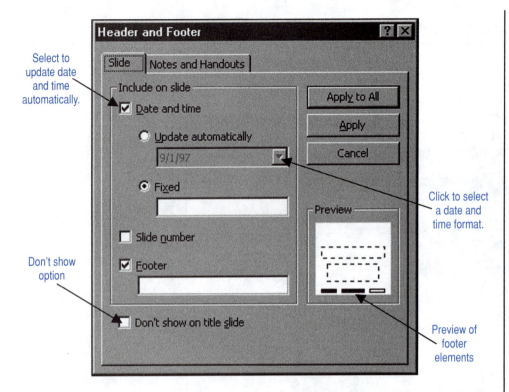

Select to update date and time automatically.

Click to select a date and time format.

Don't show option

Preview of footer elements

- If you wish to include the date and time or just the time and have it update automatically each time the presentation is accessed, click the Update automatically option. Then click the list arrow to select a desired format for the date and/or time. To insert a date and/or time that does not change, select Fixed and type the date/time you want displayed.

- If you do not wish to have slide numbers, the date and time, or any other footer text appear on the title slide, select the Don't show on title slide option.

- Since the Slide Master contains the default settings for the format of a slide, date and time, page number and footer placeholders have already been created and positioned on it by PowerPoint. *(See Slide Master illustration on page 68.)* The preview window in the Header and Footer dialog box also lets you see how these items appear on the slide. The date and time appear on the bottom left of the slide, footer text appears in the middle of the slide and the slide number appears on the bottom right of the slide.

- If you wish to change the location of any of these items on the slide, you must make the changes on the Slide Master. To move the page number, for example, select the page number placeholder (so handles appear) and drag it to a new location on the Slide Master. If you wish to center the page number on the bottom of the slide, delete the footer placeholder and move the page number placeholder into the bottom center position.

- You may format the page number, date and time, and footer text just as you would all other text within a text placeholder.

- The actual slide number will appear on your slides when you print and during a slide show. *(Presenting slide shows will be covered in Exercise 14.)*

Format Bullets

- Many AutoLayout formats include bulleted body text. The bullet styles and shapes are set in the Slide Master. You can change the bullet style, size, and shape individually for each bulleted item on each slide, or you can save time and keep the format consistent by formatting bullets on the Slide Master. Bullets formatted individually after the Slide Master has been created will override formatting set in the Slide Master.

Although bullets are usually thought to be circles or asterisks, any symbol can be used as a bullet. Fanciful symbols add visual interest to a presentation.

Slide Master

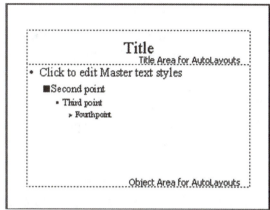

- If you wish to include text below bulleted items but would prefer no bullet on the explanatory text, you can remove the bullets. Click the Bullet On/Off button on the Formatting toolbar to turn bullets on and off on individual items or on selected text. You can also turn the bullet feature on or off by selecting or deselecting the Use a Bullet check box in the Bullet dialog box.

- To change the format and size of bullets, display the slide or Slide Master and position the insertion point in the bulleted item or bullet list level you want to change. Then select Bullet from the Format menu or right-click the mouse and select Bullet from the shortcut menu. (If the insertion point is not positioned in bulleted text and no bulleted items are selected, this option will not be available.)

- In the Bullet dialog box that appears, select a desired bullet shape, Size, and Color.

Click to select a different symbol font.

Click to turn on/off bullets.

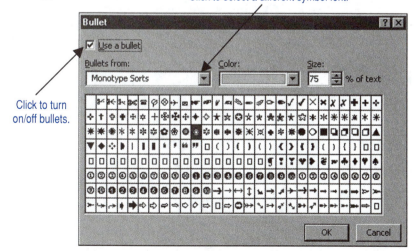

- You can select a bullet style from several character sets containing symbols and shapes (Wingdings, SymbolsA, etc). Click the Bullets from drop-down list box and select a symbol font to use.

In Part I of this exercise, you will create a template using slide masters to add graphics, change bullets, and insert page numbers. In Part II of this exercise, you will use your new template to create a presentation.

EXERCISE DIRECTIONS

PART I

1. Create a new presentation based on the **Serene** template.

2. Click Cancel in the New Slide dialog box.

3. Switch to Title Master view.

4. Format the title master as follows (see Illustration A):

    a. Insert Strategy Harmony clip. Size and position as shown.

    b. Right-align master title text.

    c. Format slide color scheme:

        -   On Custom tab, change title text to red. Click the Apply to All button.

5. Switch to Slide Master view.

6. Format slide master as follows (see Illustration B):

    a. Insert slide numbers into Number Area.

    b. Insert the following text in the Footer Area: Consensus*Harmony*Teamwork.

    c. Check the Don't show on title slide check box option. Click the Apply to All button.

    d. Format the bullets:

        -   Keep the existing colors

        -   Change shapes to Wingdings as follows:

            | First level | check mark |
            | Second level | arrow |

    e. Right-align master title text.

7. Switch to Slide view.

8. Save the presentation as a presentation template; name it **PUZZLE**.

    ✓   *Be sure to select Presentation Template from the Save as type drop-down list.*

9. Close the presentation.

PART II

1. Begin a new presentation based on the Puzzle template.

2. Insert a title slide and type the text shown in slide 1 of the Desired Results.

3. Insert a 2 Column Text slide after slide 1. Type the text shown.

4. Insert a Clip Art & Text slide after Slide 2. Enter the title and the bulleted information shown. Insert any relevant clip art graphic.

5. Insert a Text & Clip Art slide after slide 3. Type text as shown. Insert any relevant clip art graphic.

6. Compare your presentation with the Desired Results.

7. Spell check.

8. Print the presentation as handouts with six slides per page in black and white.

9. Save the presentation; name it **EFFECT**.

10. Close the presentation.

ILLUSTRATION A

ILLUSTRATION B

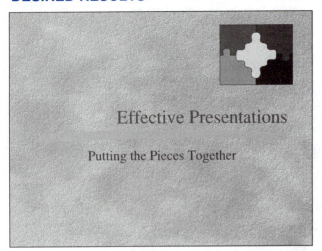

SLIDE 1

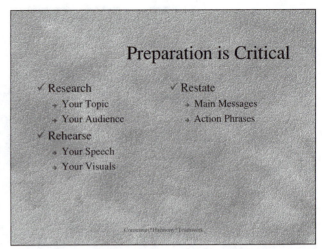

SLIDE 2

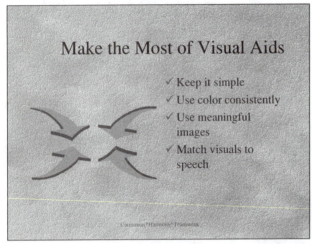

SLIDE 3

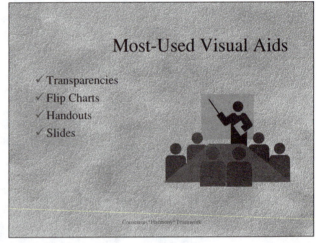

SLIDE 4

KEYSTROKES

FORMAT TEXT ON SLIDE OR TITLE MASTER

1. Open the desired presentation or create a new presentation.
2. Click **View** .... Alt + V
3. Click **Master** .... M
4. Click **Slide Master** .... S

   OR

   Click **Title Master** .... Alt + T
5. Select placeholder to change.

   OR

   Select text level to change.
6. Format font, size, alignment, enhancements, slide background, color scheme, template and other elements as desired.
7. Click 🔲 .... Alt + V , S
   to switch to Slide view.

OMIT MASTER SLIDE OBJECTS

1. Display slide on which to omit Slide Master objects.
2. Click **Format** .... Alt + O
3. Click **Background** .... K
4. Select **Omit background** .... Alt + G
   graphics from the Master.
5. Click **Apply** .... Alt + A

SAVE A PRESENTATION OR MASTER AS TEMPLATE

1. Click **File** .... Alt + F
2. Click **Save As** .... A
3. Select **Save as type** .... Alt + T
4. Select Presentation Template... ↑ ↓
5. Select **File name** .... Alt + N
6. Type a file name .... *name*
   for the template.
7. Click **Save** .... Enter

INSERT PAGE NUMBERS, DATE AND TIME, AND OTHER FOOTER TEXT

1. Click **View** .... Alt + V
2. Click **Header and Footer** .... H
3. Click **Slide** tab.
4. Click **Date and time** .... Alt + D
   to insert date and/or time.
   a. Select **Update** .... Alt + U
      automatically to have date/time update each time you open the presentation.
   b. Click the drop-down list arrow and select a date/time format.

   OR

   a. Select **Fixed** .... Alt + X
      to insert a fixed date/time.
   b. Type date/time you want ..... *date/time*
      displayed in text box.
5. Click **Slide number** .... Alt + N
   to add slide numbers.
6. Click **Footer** .... Alt + F
   and type footer text in text box, if desired.
7. Click **Don't show on** .... Alt + S
   title slide to omit footer contents on the Title slide.
8. Click **Apply to all** .... Alt + Y

   OR

   Click **Apply** .... Alt + A

   ✓ *Actual slide numbers will display when printing or during a slide show.*

TURN BULLETS ON/OFF

1. Position insertion point in bulleted item.

   OR

   Select multiple bulleted items.
2. Click the **Bullets** button ⬛ on the Formatting toolbar.

   OR

   a. Click **Format** .... Alt + O
   b. Click **Bullet** .... B
   c. Click **Use a Bullet** .... Alt + U
   d. Click **OK** .... Enter

   ✓ *An ✓ in the box beside Use a bullet indicates that the feature is active. An empty box means the feature is inactive and no bullet will appear.*

CHANGE BULLET CHARACTER

1. Position insertion point in desired bulleted item or select several bulleted items.
2. Right-click and select **Bullet** .... B
   from the shortcut menu.

   OR

   a. Click **Format** .... Alt + O
   b. Click **Bullet** .... B
3. Click **Bullets from** .... Alt + B , ↓
   list to select desired character set.
4. Select desired bullet character.
5. Click **OK** .... Enter

CHANGE BULLET SIZE/COLOR

1. Position insertion point in bulleted item to change or select several bulleted items.
2. Right-click and select **Bullet** .... B
   from the shortcut menu.

   OR

   a. Click **Format** .... Alt + O
   b. Click **Bullet** .... B

   To change bullet size:

   a. Select **Size** box .... Alt + S
      in upper right corner.
   b. Type desired percentage .... *number* of original size.

   OR

   Click 🔼 to increase or decrease bullet size.

   To change bullet color:

   c. Click in the **Color** .... Alt + C
      drop-down list box.
   d. Select the desired color.
3. Click **OK** .... Enter

Exercise 11

- **Use Slide Rulers and Guides** ■ **Floating Toolbars**
- **Draw Graphic Objects** ■ **Use AutoShapes** ■ **Create Text Objects**
- **Group and Ungroup Objects** ■ **Layer Objects**

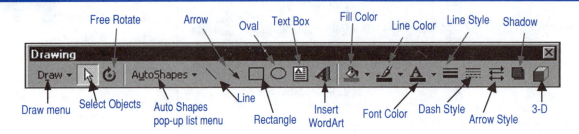

NOTES

Use Slide Rulers and Guides

- In PowerPoint, you can display a horizontal and a vertical ruler. Rulers allow you to place objects and text on the slide with more accuracy. Rulers may be displayed by selecting Ruler from the View menu.

- Ruler measurements will display differently depending on what is selected on the slide. If an object is selected, the ruler displays in *drawing mode,* and the zero point is at the center of each ruler. If text is selected, the ruler is displayed in *text mode,* and the ruler highlights the measurement of the text placeholder.

- A slide measures 10 inches wide by 7.5 inches tall. Note the screen illustrations below in which the rulers are displayed in text mode.

- As you move your mouse on the slide, a corresponding indicator displays on the ruler, showing you the horizontal and vertical position of your mouse pointer on the slide.

- **Guides** may also be displayed by selecting Guides from the View menu. Guides assist you in aligning objects or text on a slide. Note the grids in the drawing mode illustration below.

Use rulers and guides together to help you with exact placement of objects on a slide. As you move your cursor over a slide with the rulers and guides displayed, the cursor's location is indicated by a line on both the horizontal and vertical rulers.

Text Mode

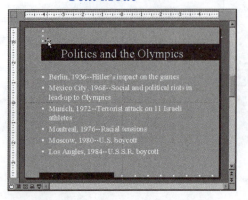

Drawing Mode

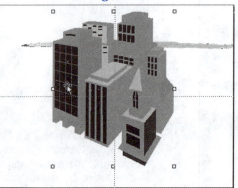

Floating Toolbars

- If a submenu appears with a move handle, you can click and drag it away from the menu while leaving it on screen to create a floating toolbar. To close a floating toolbar, click the close box on the toolbar.

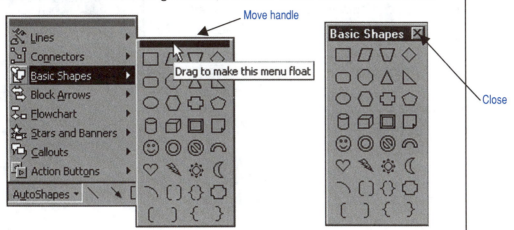

Draw Graphic Objects

- ■ **Drawing tools** are used to create simple objects or designs on your slides. Drawing tools are found on the Drawing toolbar, which displays by default.

- ■ Drawings created using the Drawing toolbar are considered objects. Objects include lines, shapes, and freehand designs. Closed shapes may be filled with a color or pattern.

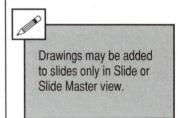

Drawings may be added to slides only in Slide or Slide Master view.

- ■ To draw an object, click the Drawing toolbar button of the shape or object you wish to draw. The insertion point changes to a crosshair $\boxed{+}$. Position the crosshair where you want to start the object. Click and drag the crosshair to the point where you want to end the object. After the object is drawn, it will appear with handles. To remove the handles, click the Select Objects tool ▨ or press the Escape key. To redisplay the handles, click the Select Objects tool and click the object.

- ■ Displaying the rulers and guides when drawing objects will allow you to determine the object's size and position in relation to the slide's size.

- ■ Some of the most commonly used tools are displayed on the Drawing toolbar:

  - Use the **Line tool** ▨ to draw a straight line. You can change the line style and color by selecting the line, then clicking the Line Style, Dash Style, Arrow Style, and/or Line Color buttons on the Drawing toolbar.

  - Use the **Arrow tool** ▨ to draw arrows. You can change the arrow style or color by selecting the arrow, clicking the Arrow Style button ▨ on the Drawing toolbar, then selecting a different style. To change the color of the arrow, click More Arrows on the Arrow Style button pop-up menu and select a new Color.

  - Use the **Rectangle tool** ▨ to draw squares or rectangles. To draw a perfect square, hold down the Shift key while dragging the mouse, and release the mouse button before releasing the Shift key.

  - Use the **Oval tool** ▨ to draw circles or ovals. To draw a perfect circle, hold down the Shift key while dragging the mouse, and as with the Rectangle tool, be sure to release the mouse button before releasing the Shift key.

Use AutoShapes

- When you select **AutoShapes** on the Drawing toolbar, several menus containing a variety of shapes (lines, connectors, flowchart elements, callouts, etc.) display. As mentioned earlier, each menu can be dragged away from the pop-up menu so you can quickly access it. Below is an illustration and explanation of each category available on the AutoShapes menu.

Lines

Create curves, freeform, and scribble lines. The straight line and arrow and double arrow tools are also available on this menu.

Connectors

Connect objects using a straight, angled (elbow), or curved line. Connector lines stay attached to objects when objects are rearranged. You may use straight lines arrows as connectors.

Basic Shapes

Allows you to draw common geometric shapes as well as more playful forms (Smiley Face, "No" Symbol, Heart, Lightning Bolt, Sun, Moon) and brackets and braces.

Block Arrows

Includes various arrow shapes as well as arrow callout options.

Flowchart

New feature in PowerPoint 97. Allows you to quickly and efficiently build flowcharts with 28 standard shapes.

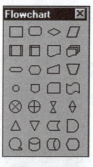

Stars and Banners

This AutoShape option includes button tools for explosions, stars, ribbons, scrolls, and waves.

To change the shape of an AutoShape:

- Select the shape you wish to change.
- Click **Draw**.
- Click **Change AutoShape**.
- Select a new AutoShape from one of the categories.

Callouts

Create callouts visually appropriate to the mood and style of your presentation. See also the arrow callout options in the Block Arrows AutoShapes pop-up menu.

Action Buttons

Use to create a presentation for the Internet. Navigation buttons like Home, Help, Back, Next, etc., will help your viewers navigate your presentation.

- To draw an AutoShape, click the desired shape from the pop-up submenu palette of shapes. Then, click and drag the mouse to expand the shape to the desired size. The color of the shape may then be changed by selecting the shape with the Select Objects tool, and clicking the **Fill Color** button ![icon] on the Drawing toolbar.

Create Text Objects

- Text entered on slides thus far has been entered into placeholders. Text added using the **Text Box tool** ![icon] on the Drawing toolbar creates a separate object that can be moved, sized, deleted, etc., without affecting text in placeholders.

- Use the **Text Box tool** to add text to pictures or other objects, including placeholders.

- After selecting the Text Box tool, outline the area of the slide that the text should occupy using the procedures you used to draw a rectangle. The text box will expand downward as you enter text.

Group and Ungroup Objects

- When a drawing is comprised of several basic shapes, it is difficult to move, copy, or duplicate all the shapes as a whole object. **Grouping** allows you to select all the shapes in the group and treat them as whole objects so that copying, duplicating, and moving them becomes possible.

- To group an object comprised of individual shapes, select each shape. (Hold the Shift key down while you click each shape.) Select Group from the pop-up Draw menu. You can undo the grouped objects by selecting Ungroup from the Draw menu. You can also use the shortcut menu to execute these commands.

Layer Objects

- Shapes may be layered or stacked on top of each other to create interesting effects. You may adjust the layers by moving them back or bringing them forward in the stack. To adjust the layers of shapes or objects, click the shape or object and select Order, Send to Back or Bring to Front from the Draw menu. This feature may also be accessed via the Shortcut menu.

To draw an AutoShape:

Click **AutoShapes** pop-up button on Drawing toolbar.

Click desired shape from pop up menu:

- Lines
- Connectors
- Basic Shapes
- Block Arrows
- Flowchart
- Stars and Banners
- Callouts
- Action Buttons

To group an object:
- Hold down **Shift** while clicking objects to group.
- Click **Draw**.
- Click **Group**.

To ungroup an object:
- Select desired grouped object.
- Click **Draw**.
- Click **Ungroup**.

> *In this exercise, you will create a logo on the slide master using the AutoShapes menu and the Text Box button on the Drawing toolbar. You will then view each slide in your presentation to see the new effects. See Desired Results on the next page.*

EXERCISE DIRECTIONS

1. Open ⌨**WPRT**, or open 💾**11WPRT**.
2. Move to slide 2. Switch to Slide Master view:

   a. Insert Explosion 2 AutoShape in the lower-left corner of the slide.

   ✓ *Do not become frustrated if the AutoShape does not appear exactly as shown in the illustration. AutoShapes require a great deal of manipulation—you can do this easily by dragging the handles of the AutoShape handles after the initial placement of the image. For now, simply concentrate on making the Explosion 2 AutoShape accommodate the text typed in step C, without expanding the text box.*

   b. Change the file color of the Explosion 2 AutoShape to a color lighter than the selected orange.

   c. Using the Text Box tool, create a text placeholder in the Explosion 2 AutoShape, and insert *On the Air!* in any desired black font.

   d. Manipulate the Explosion 2 AutoShape so that the text is in place and both elements look in balance with each other.

   e. Insert a lightning bolt from AutoShapes Basic Shapes submenu palette. Color the lightning bolt blue.

   f. Modify graphic and text elements as necessary until you are satisfied that the image looks complete.

   g. Group all three elements.

3. Display slide rulers and guides, if necessary.
4. Delete the Date Area placeholder from the slide master.
5. Expand the Footer Area placeholder to the left margin—where the previous Date Area placeholder began.
6. Enter the following footer text in the Footer Area placeholder: Bringing the World to You!
7. Left align footer text. Increase font size as appropriate, and check the Don't show on title Slide check box option.
8. Switch to Slide view.
9. Switch slide 4 layout to Clip Art & Text. Adjust fonts as necessary.
10. Print one copy as handouts with six slides per page in black and white.
11. Close the file; save the changes.

ILLUSTRATION A

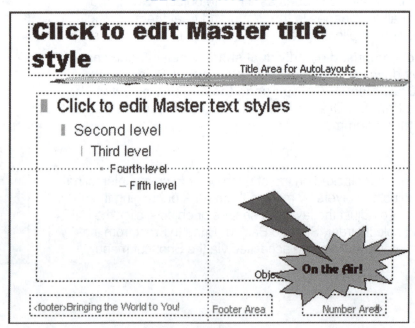

DESIRED RESULTS

WPRT Television

Management Team
Annual Meeting

SLIDE 1

Agenda

▌ The Year in Review
▌ Programming Projections
▌ The Fall Forecast
▌ New Affiliates

Bringing the World to You!

SLIDE 2

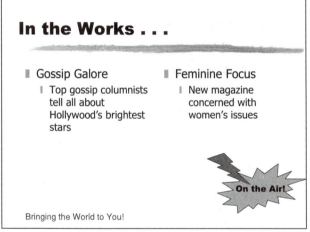

In the Works . . .

▌ Gossip Galore
  ▎ Top gossip columnists tell all about Hollywood's brightest stars

▌ Feminine Focus
  ▎ New magazine concerned with women's issues

Bringing the World to You!

SLIDE 3

Programming Projections

▌ Programming Success
  ▎ The Hollies
  ▎ Moon Rock
  ▎ Just Plain Folk

Bringing the World to You!

SLIDE 4

Continued…

New Employees

- Jane Susans, Production Assistant
- Kenneth Coleman, Sound Specialist
- Jerry Gomez, Sports Announcer

On the Air!

Bringing the World to You!

SLIDE 5

Programs Replaced

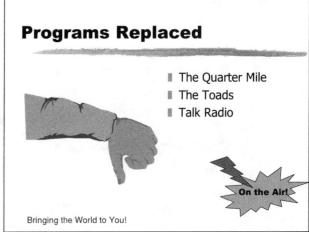

- The Quarter Mile
- The Toads
- Talk Radio

On the Air!

Bringing the World to You!

SLIDE 6

WPRT Syndicated Shows

- The Morning Commute
- Rock Block
- Street Beat
- Sounds of Jazz

On the Air!

Bringing the World to You!

SLIDE 7

The Year in Review

- Organizational Changes
- Sales Records
- Ratings Review

On the Air!

Bringing the World to You!

SLIDE 8

KEYSTROKES

DISPLAY RULER AND/OR GUIDES

1. Click **V**iew .... `Alt`+`V`
2. Click **R**uler .... `R`
   AND/OR
   Click **G**uides .... `G`

DRAW AUTOSHAPES

1. Click **A**utoShapes
   pop-up button .... `Alt`+`U`
   on Drawing toolbar.
2. Click desired shape from pop-up
   menu:
   - **L**ines .... `L`
   - Co**n**nectors .... `N`
   - **B**asic Shapes .... `B`
   - Block **A**rrows .... `A`
   - **F**lowchart .... `F`
   - **S**tars and Banners .... `S`
   - **C**allouts .... `C`
   - Action Butt**o**ns .... `O`
3. Position crosshair `+` at point where
   shape will start.
4. Click and drag to desired end point.
   ✓ *Drawing shapes usually require
   the same procedure. You click
   and drag the mouse point to the
   right and down. Some shapes
   require additional actions to get
   the desired result. The distance
   and drag direction determine the
   size and shape of the object.*

DRAW PERFECT CIRCLE/SQUARE

1. Click `▢` or `⬭` on Drawing toolbar.
2. Position crosshair `+` at point where
   shape will start.
3. Press **Shift** key while dragging mouse
   diagonally to desired end point.
4. Release mouse button.
5. Release **Shift** key.

DRAW ARROWS

1. Click arrow button `↖` on Drawing
   toolbar.
2. Position crosshair `+` at start point.
3. Click to drag to end point.

DRAW CURVES

1. Click `AutoShapes ▾` .... `Alt`+`U`
   on Drawing toolbar.
2. Click **L**ines .... `L`
   on pop-up menu.
3. Click and hold mouse as you drag the
   pointer in the desired direction.
4. Move pointer to draw shape, clicking
   to change direction or angle, if
   necessary.
5. Double-click to stop drawing.

CREATE TEXT OBJECTS

1. Click **Text Box** button `🄰` on
   Drawing toolbar.
2. Position text cursor `↓` at text start
   point.
3. Click and drag to form confined text box.

GROUP OBJECTS

1. Hold down **Shift** while clicking objects
   to group.
2. Click **D**raw.......................... `Alt`+`R`
3. Click **G**roup................................. `G`

UNGROUP OBJECTS

1. Select desired grouped object.
2. Click **D**raw.......................... `Alt`+`R`
3. Click **U**ngroup .... `U`

REGROUP OBJECTS

*Regroups most recently ungrouped
object. If slide containing ungrouped
object becomes inactive, object cannot
be regrouped using this procedure. It
will have to be grouped.*

1. Click **D**raw.......................... `Alt`+`R`
2. Click Reg**r**oup............................. `O`

LAYER OBJECTS

1. Select desired object.
2. Click **D**raw.......................... `Alt`+`R`
3. Click **O**rder................................. `R`
4. Click Send **B**ackward .... `B`
   to send object back one layer.
   OR
   Click Bring **F**orward.................... `F`
   to send object forward one layer.
5. Repeat step 4 until object is properly
   placed.

OR

1. Select desired object.
2. Right-click selected object.
3. Click **O**rder................................. `R`
4. Select desired option:

OPTION	MOVEMENT
Bring to Front	Places objects on top of all other objects.
Send to Back	Places object beneath all other objects.
Bring Forward	Moves object one layer up on the stack.
Send Backward	Moves object one layer down on the stack.

CYCLE THROUGH OBJECTS

1. Press **Ctrl + A** .... `Ctrl`+`A`
   to select all objects.
2. Press **Tab**................................. `Tab`
   until desired object is selected.

Exercise

12

■ **Summary**

In this exercise, you will create a template and then apply it to a presentation created in an earlier exercise.

EXERCISE DIRECTIONS

PART I

1. Create a new blank presentation.
2. Click Cancel in the New Slide dialog box.
3. Switch to Slide Master view. Insert a new title master (Insert, New Title Ma<u>s</u>ter).
4. Display the guides, ruler, and Drawing toolbar.
5. View title master:
   a. Move and size the Master title style placeholder as shown in Illustration A on the next page.
   b. Italicize the Master title style placeholder and color it red.
6. Switch to Slide Master view:
   a. Color the Master title style placeholder red.
   b. Create five perfect circles and arrange them approximately as shown in Illustration B on the next page.
      - Color the outlines white.
      - Fill the largest circle dark green.
      - Fill each subsequent circle a shade lighter than the previous one.
7. Group the circles and copy the grouped object.
8. Switch to Master Title view.
   - Paste the grouped object. Position and size it as shown in the Illustration.
9. Save the presentation as a template; name it **BOUNCE**.

PART II

1. Open ⌨**WPRT**, or open 💾**12WPRT**.
2. Switch to Slide view.
3. Apply the Bounce template to the presentation.
4. Display slide 3 (In the Works...)
   - Insert the following text:
     a. Space Watch (title)
     b. The first Cyber-Soap Opera (subtitle)
5. Insert the date in the footer.
6. Print one copy as handouts with three slides per page in black and white.
7. Close the presentation; save the changes.

ILLUSTRATION A (Title Master)

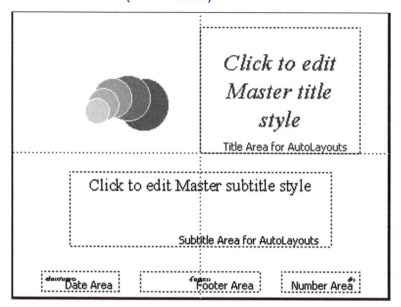

ILLUSTRATION B (Slide Master)

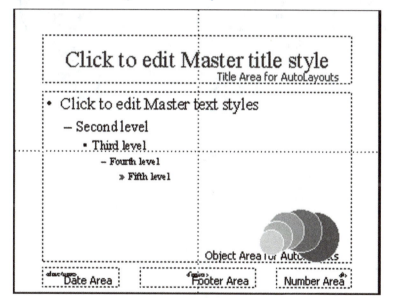

WPRT
Television

Management Team
Annual Meeting

SLIDE 1

Agenda

- The Year in Review
- Programming Projections
- The Fall Forecast
- New Affiliates

September 26, 1997   Bringing the World to You!

SLIDE 2

In the Works . . .

- Gossip Galore
  - Top gossip columnists tell all about Hollywood's brightest stars

- Feminine Focus
  - New magazine concerned with women's issues
- Space Watch
  - The first Cyber-Soap Opera

September 26, 1997   Bringing the World to You!

SLIDE 3

Programming Projections

- Programming Success
  - The Hollies
  - Moon Rock
  - Just Plain Folk

September 26, 1997   Bringing the World to You!

SLIDE 4

Continued…

New Employees

- Jane Susans, Production Assistant
- Kenneth Coleman, Sound Specialist
- Jerry Gomez, Sports Announcer

September 26, 1997   Bringing the World to You!

SLIDE 5

Programs Replaced

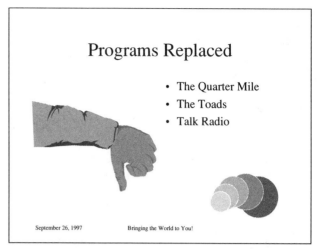

- The Quarter Mile
- The Toads
- Talk Radio

September 26, 1997   Bringing the World to You!

SLIDE 6

WPRT Syndicated Shows

- The Morning Commute
- Rock Block
- Street Beat
- Sounds of Jazz

September 26, 1997   Bringing the World to You!

SLIDE 7

The Year in Review

- Organizational Changes
- Sales Records
- Ratings Review

September 26, 1997   Bringing the World to You!

SLIDE 8

87

■ **Summary**

In this exercise, you will create a new presentation using a predesigned template, change views, add clip art, change slide position and formatting, print out one copy as a handout and save it.

EXERCISE DIRECTIONS

1. Create a new presentation using the Fans template.

2. Click Cancel in the New Slide dialog box.

3. Switch to Title Master view.

4. Move the Master title style placeholder to the top right of the slide and the Master Subtitle style placeholder to the bottom right.

5. Change the master title text to blue and the subtitle text to a yellow 40-point font.

6. View slide master.

7. Change the master title text to 54 point. Center the text.

8. Change all bullets to a star shape.

9. Switch to Slide view and insert a Title Slide.

10. Type the following text in the title placeholder: Globetrotters Travel

11. Type the following text in the sub-title placeholder: The Perfect Getaway.

12. Switch to Outline view and type the outline shown to the right.

13. Switch to Slide view.

14. Apply the appropriate slide AutoLayouts and clip art shown in Desired Result.

15. Increase the font size of the bulleted text on slides 2, 5, and 6 to 36 points.

16. Switch to Slide Sorter view and review the presentation.

17. Spell check the presentation.

18. Print one copy as handouts (6 slides per page) in Black and white.

19. Close the presentation; name it **VACATION**.

1 | *Rest and Relax*
   - Beautiful Beaches
   - Seawater Pools
   - Massage Therapy
   - Daily Meditation

2 | *Invigorating Activities*
   - Daily Nature Walks
   - Volcano Hikes
   - Scuba Diving
   - Surfing
   - Sailing

3 | *Romance*
   - Picnics
   - Four-Star Restaurants
   - Honeymoon Packages

4 | *Meet People*
   - Tennis Tournaments
   - Volleyball Games
   - Dance Contests
   - Barbecues

5 | *Let Us Take Care of You*
   - Attentive, Experienced Staff
   - Babysitting Services
   - Airport Transportation

DESIRED RESULTS

SLIDE 1

SLIDE 2

SLIDE 3

SLIDE 4

SLIDE 5

SLIDE 6

Next Lesson

Lesson 3

Work with Slide Shows

Exercises 14-20

- Show a Presentation
- Add Transitions, Sound, and Timing
- Animate Text and Objects
- Animation Effects Toolbar
- Preset Animation for Bulleted Lists
- Custom Animation
- PowerPoint Central
- The Annotator
- Create Continuously Running Presentations
- Set Up a Slide Show
- Create Note Pages and Handouts
- Speaker Notes
- Notes Master and Handout Master
- Pack and Go
- Meeting Minder

Exercise 14

■ **Show a Presentation** ■ **Checking Slides Before the Presentation**
■ **Add Slide Transitions** ■ **Set Transition Effect Speed** ■ **Add Sound**
■ **Set Transition Advance** ■ **Rehearse Timings** ■ **Add Timings**

NOTES

Show a Presentation

- PowerPoint enables you to show an on-screen presentation of your slides to an audience.

- When a slide show is presented, each slide displays on the entire screen without showing the PowerPoint program (toolbars and menus).

- You can change slides by clicking the mouse or pressing a key.

- To activate a slide show, display the first slide to be shown, then click the Slide Show button on the lower left of the screen, or select Slide Sho<u>w</u> from the <u>V</u>iew menu.

Checking Slides Before the Presentation

- The **Style Checker** feature within PowerPoint lets you check your slides for spelling errors, visual clarity (too many font styles used), and inconsistencies in case and punctuation before running the slide show. To do so, select St<u>y</u>le Checker from the <u>T</u>ools menu. In the Style Checker dialog box that follows, select the options you wish PowerPoint to check for and click the <u>S</u>tart button.

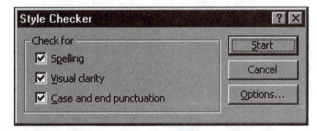

- After checking the presentation, the Style Checker Summary dialog box appears and PowerPoint displays a summary of its findings. You may then return to your presentation to make changes.

Slides may be shown one at a time as an oral report is given, or they may run continuously. The run continuously option is convenient if you want, for example, to have a demonstration at a trade show.

If you plan to show your slide presentation to a large audience, you will need to project the computer image onto a large screen. This will require a projection device. See your local computer dealer for projection device information.

To show a Presentation:
- Open desired presentation.
- Click **Slide Show** button .

OR
- Click **View**.
- Click **Slide Show**.

Add Slide Transitions

- **Transitions** control the way slides move on and off the screen.

- Transitions may be added to slides in all views, but Slide Sorter view offers the quickest and easiest way to add transitions because the Slide Sorter toolbar contains tools for performing these tasks.

Click to select a transition effect.

Rehearse Timings button

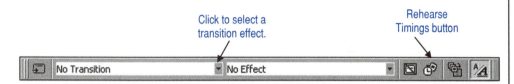

- To add a transition in Slide Sorter view, click the list arrow next to the Slide Transition list box. A drop-down menu of transition choices appears. Select a transition effect. Slides displayed in Slide Sorter view contain transitions that are marked by a slide icon, which appears below and to the left of the miniature slide image.

Transition indicator

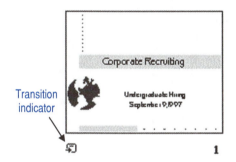

1

2

- To add transitions to slides in views other than Slide Sorter, select Slide Transition from the Slide Show menu. In the Slide Transition dialog box that follows, you can select a transition effect, the speed of the transition and how you wish to advance the slide (manually–On mouse click, or Automatically–after a specified number of seconds).

Effect preview window

Transition effect speed

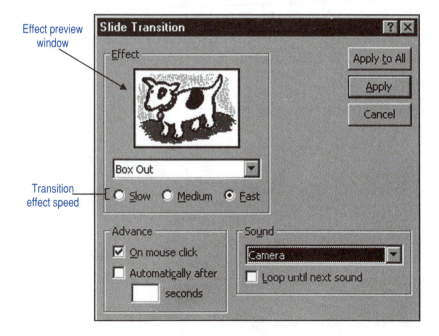

- Transitions include a number of special effects. Select a transition effect and note the result in the Effect preview window. A description of each of the transition effects appears below.

Blinds	Creates an effect of opening and closing venetian blinds and can be set for horizontal or vertical.
Box	Forms a box and opens from the center outward or the edges inward.
Checkerboard	Creates a checkerboard effect by placing small black squares randomly on the screen to reveal the new slide. This option can also be set for horizontal (Across) or vertical (Down).
Cover	Replaces the displaced slide with the next slide moving from a specified direction. There are eight directional options for this transitional effect.
Cut	Replaces the slide with the next slide without directional motion.
Dissolve	Sprinkles the slide on and off the screen.
Fade Through Black	Gradually darkens the displaced slide to black before revealing the next slide.
Random Bars	Reveals the new slide gradually by placing horizontal or vertical bars on the screen.
Split	Reveals and removes a slide from the center outward or inward, horizontally or vertically.
Strips	Reveals and removes a slide from one corner of the screen to the other using any one of four directions.
Uncover	Reveals a new slide as the active slide is removed. There are eight directional options for this transitional effect.
Wipe	Removes displaced slide from the screen in the specified direction, revealing the new slide. There are four directional options to choose from.
Random Transition	Assigns a random transition effect as you move from slide to slide. Assigning Random Transition to numerous slides generates a random assortment of transitions.

Set Transition Effect Speed

- You can adjust the speed of the transition effect by clicking Slow, Medium, or Fast in the Slide Transition dialog box.

Add Sound

- In addition to adding a visual transition for moving slides on and off screen, you may add a sound effect to play during transitions. If you want the sound to affect one slide, select the slide to receive the sound effect, then select the effect from the Sound drop-down list box in the Slide Transition dialog box.

- If you wish the sound to remain until the next sound effect is encountered on a slide, click the Loop until next sound check box.

Set Transition Advance

- The Slide Transition dialog box Advance option allows you to specify how you wish to advance from one slide to the next. Select <u>O</u>n mouse click to manually advance the slide, or select Automati<u>c</u>ally to have PowerPoint advance the slide for you. If you choose Automati<u>c</u>ally, however, you must specify the number of seconds you wish the slide to remain on screen before PowerPoint advances to the next slide.

- If you select an automatic advance, the timing you assign to the slide will appear below the slide in Slide Sorter view.

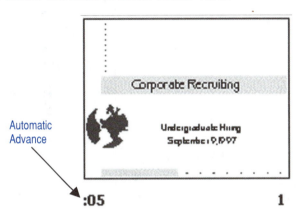

Automatic
Advance

:05   1

- Advance timings may be set individually for each slide or collectively for all slides. Slides containing timings may, however, be advanced manually when necessary.

Rehearse Timings

- The **Rehearse Timings** feature allows you to rehearse your presentation and set the advance timings for each slide as you do so. To rehearse a presentation, select <u>R</u>ehearse Timings from the Sli<u>d</u>e Show menu, or click the Rehearse Timings button 🔄 on the toolbar in Slide Sorter view. A slide show will begin with the following Rehearsal dialog box appearing on the screen. Click the advance button to stop the timing on one slide and restart it for the next slide.

Elapsed time   Restarts timing for   Elapsed time
of slide show   individual slide   of current slide

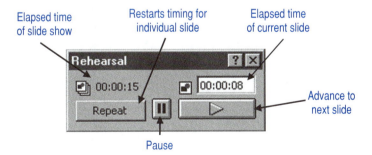

Advance to
next slide

Pause

Add Timings

- **Timings** control the speed with which slides replace other slides. Setting a time tells PowerPoint how long the slide will remain on the screen.

- Timings may be included as part of the transition. Timings are set in seconds, with .03 representing three seconds.

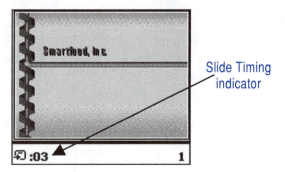

Slide Timing indicator

- Timings may be set individually for each slide or collectively for all slides. Slides containing timings may, however, be advanced manually when necessary. Timings may be set using the Slide Transition dialog box in Slide view, Outline view, or Slide Sorter view. Slide timings display to the right of the transition slide icon in Slide Sorter view.

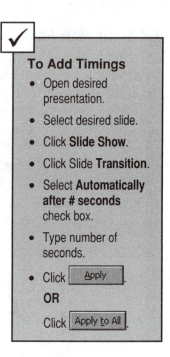

To Add Timings

- Open desired presentation.
- Select desired slide.
- Click **Slide Show**.
- Click Slide **Transition**.
- Select **Automatically after # seconds** check box.
- Type number of seconds.
- Click Apply .

  OR

  Click Apply to All .

In this exercise, you will edit a previously created presentation by inserting a new slide and adding transitions and timings to the slides. View your slide presentation and see Desired Results on the next page.

EXERCISE DIRECTIONS

1. Open 🎞️**EFFECT**, or open 💾**14EFFECT**.

2. Insert a new slide at the end of the presentation. Enter the following text:

   Know Your Audience

   - Will it be a large or small audience?
   - Who will you be speaking to?
   - Is the subject you will be discussing new to the people in the audience?

3. Run Style Checker. Compare result with Desired Results.

   ✓ *When the **Case and end punctuation** option is checked in the Style Checker dialog box, Style Checker will change the capitalization options in your presentation without presenting you with a dialog box to approve or reject individual changes. In most cases, this change is fine and does not disrupt the presentation; in some cases, however, you must change the capitalization manually after the style checker procedure has been completed.*

4. Run the slide show.

5. Switch to Slide Sorter view.

6. Add the following transitions to the slides using the Slide Sorter toolbar:

Slide 1 (title slide)	Checkerboard Across
Slide 2 (Preparation is Critical)	Box Out
Slide 4 (Most Often Used Visual Aids)	Blinds Vertical

7. Add the following transitions using the Slide Transitions dialog box:

Slide 3 (Make the Most of Visual Aids)	Dissolve
Slide 5 (Know Your Audience)	Wipe Right

8. Set a automatic advance of 5 seconds for all the slides.

9. Run the slide show again; note the transitions.

10. Close the file; save the changes.

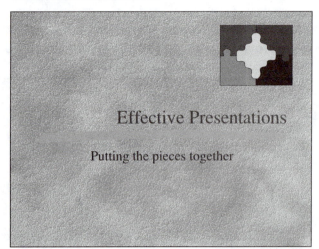

Effective Presentations

Putting the pieces together

SLIDE 1

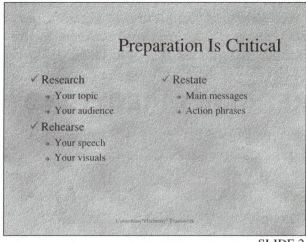

Preparation Is Critical

✓ Research
  → Your topic
  → Your audience
✓ Rehearse
  → Your speech
  → Your visuals

✓ Restate
  → Main messages
  → Action phrases

Consensus*Harmony*Teamwork

SLIDE 2

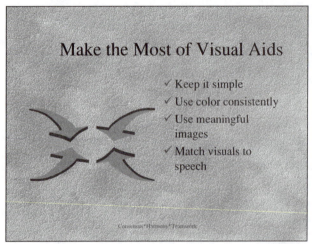

Make the Most of Visual Aids

✓ Keep it simple
✓ Use color consistently
✓ Use meaningful images
✓ Match visuals to speech

Consensus*Harmony*Teamwork

SLIDE 3

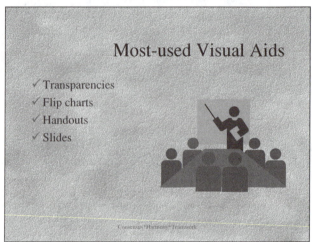

Most-used Visual Aids

✓ Transparencies
✓ Flip charts
✓ Handouts
✓ Slides

Consensus*Harmony*Teamwork

SLIDE 4

Know Your Audience

✓ Will it be a large or small audience?
✓ Who will you be speaking to?
✓ Is the subject you will be discussing new to the people in the audience?

Consensus*Harmony*Teamwork

SLIDE 5

KEYSTROKES

CHECKING SLIDES BEFORE THE PRESENTATION

1. Open desired presentation.
2. Click **Tools** .... `Alt` + `T`
3. Click **Style Checker** .... `Y`
4. Click desired options.
5. Click [Start] .... `Enter`

SHOW PRESENTATION

1. Open desired presentation.
2. Click **Slide Show** button .... 🖵

   OR

   a. Click **View** .... `Alt` + `V`

   b. Click **Slide Show** .... `W`

ADVANCE SLIDES

1. Start presentation.
2. Click left mouse button.

   OR

   Press **Enter** .... `Enter`

ADD TRANSITION

Slide Sorter View

1. View desired slide in Slide Sorter view.
2. Click [No Transition ▾] on Slide Sorter toolbar to display a list of effects.

   OR

   Click **Slide Transition** button 🔲 on Slide Sorter toolbar, and click **Effect** drop-down list.

3. Select desired transitions.
4. Click [Apply] .... `Enter`

   OR

   Click [Apply to All] .... `Alt` + `T`

Any View

✓ *The following command is available in Slide, Slide Sorter, Outline, and Notes Page views.*

1. Display desired slide.
2. Click **Slide Show** .... `Alt` + `D`
3. Click **Slide Transition** .... `T`

   ✓ *No transition options are available until a transition effect is selected.*

4. Select desired transition from **Effect** drop-down list box.
5. Select desired speed for transition:
   - **Slow** .... `Alt` + `S`
   - **Medium** .... `Alt` + `M`
   - **Fast** .... `Alt` + `F`
6. Select desired Advance method:
   a. **On mouse click** .... `Alt` + `O`
   b. **Automatically after # seconds** and type number of seconds .... *number*
7. Select desired **Sound** .... `Alt` + `U` effect from drop-down list box.
8. Click [Apply] .... `Enter`

   OR

   Click [Apply to All] .... `Alt` + `T`

SET SLIDE TIMINGS

1. Open desired presentation.
2. Select desired slide.
3. Click **Slide Show** .... `Alt` + `D`
4. Click **Slide Transition** .... `T`
5. Select **Automatically** .... `Alt` + `C` **after # seconds** check box.
6. Type number of seconds .... *number*
7. Click [Apply] .... `Enter`

   OR

   Click [Apply to All] .... `Alt` + `T`

Exercise 15

- ■ **Animate Text and Objects** ■ **Animation Effects Toolbar**
- ■ **Animation for Bulleted Lists** ■ **Custom Animation**
- ■ **PowerPoint Central**

NOTES

Animate Text and Objects

- ■ In addition to creating a variety of transitions from slide to slide, you can use PowerPoint's animation functions to control the way text and objects appear on a slide show. For example, on a slide with bulleted text, you can display the entire list all at once or one bulleted item at a time. During the slide show, the items in the list appear when you click the mouse or at the time you designate. Displaying the contents of a bulleted list one at a time is frequently referred to as a **build**.

- ■ You can also apply animation to objects, such as charts and clip art, using the Custom Animation dialog box. Using this dialog box, you can assign an effect, arrange the order of the animation, determine the timing (when the effect will activate), and preview your settings.

Animation Effects Toolbar

- ■ The Animation Effects toolbar lets you apply effects to individual parts of slides. You can use this toolbar in Slide, Slide Sorter, and Notes Page views; however, many of the functions are available only in Slide view.

- ■ Click the <u>V</u>iew menu and select <u>T</u>oolbars. Select Animation Effects to turn on the toolbar. You can also click on the **Animation Effects** button on the Formatting toolbar. The Animation Effects button is not available if you are in Slide Sorter view.

✓

To animate an object:

- • Click **Slide Show**.
- • Click **Custom Animation**.
- • Select the object that you wish to animate.
- • Select from the **Entry animation and sound** drop-down list box under the **Effects** tab.

Animation for Bulleted Lists

- To apply entry animation to bulleted lists, display the Animation Effects toolbar and switch to Slide view. Select the slide to which you want to apply animation, and click in the bulleted list on the slide. Click the desired entry animation effect to the bulleted list. Sound effects accompany many of the preset animation effects.

- You can also apply animation build effects to slides by selecting Preset Animation from the Slide Show menu. Select the desired animation, or turn the current animation Off.

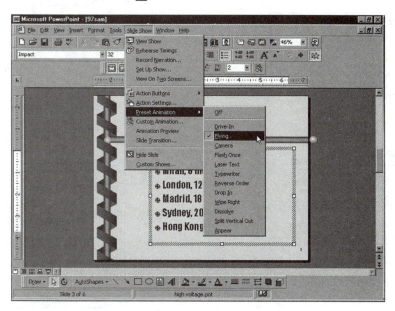

- To preview how the text will appear in the slide show, click Slide Show on the menu and select Animation Preview. A miniature slide will display how the slide will appear during a slide show. Click the close box to remove the miniature from the screen. You can also click the Slide Show button at the bottom left of the screen. Press the Escape key to return to the previous view.

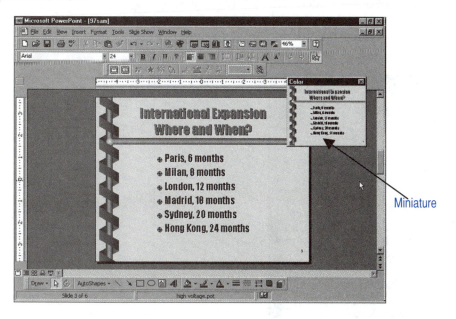

Miniature

Custom Animation

- In the Custom Animation dialog box, you can control a variety of animation effects and apply them to different elements on a slide, including charts and clip art.
- Switch to Slide view and select the slide to which you want to apply animation. Then, click Slide Show on the menu and select Custom Animation. In the Custom Animation dialog box that follows, choose the element you wish to animate.

Selected slide element

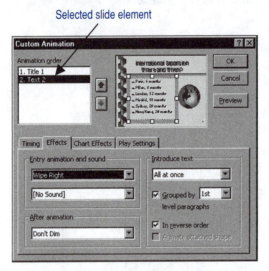

You can preview animation effects in the Custom Animation dialog box by clicking on the Preview button.

To apply custom animation:

- Switch to **Slide view**. Select the slide to which you want to apply animation.
- Click **Slide Show** on the menu.
- Select **Custom Animation**.
- In the dialog box that follows, choose the element you wish to animate.

- Below and on the following page is an explanation of the animation options. Options that are available depend on the object or text item that you are animating.

  - **Animation order** Displays a list of objects that have been animated and the order in which they will appear. To change the order, select the item you want to move and click the arrows to the right of the Animation order box.

  - **Timing tab** Displays objects that are not animated on the selected slide. Select an object, text, chart, or title to animate from the list. Select the Animate radio button to apply effects. The default timing allows for the effect to start when you click the mouse. If you click Automatically, you can specify the number of seconds that you want the effect to wait after the previous event.

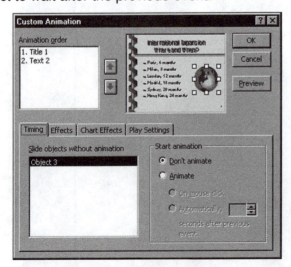

- **Effects tab** Lets you determine the way an element will display, apply a sound effect, adjust how the element appears after the animation, how much the element is displayed, even reverse the order of, for example, a bulleted list. Some of these options will not be available if you are working with an object, however.

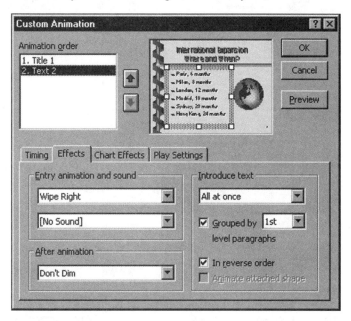

- **Chart Effects tab** Allows you to animate sections of a chart. The chart will appear all at once or by category. For example, a pie chart could appear piece by piece. You can also determine how the sections will appear and add sound effects.

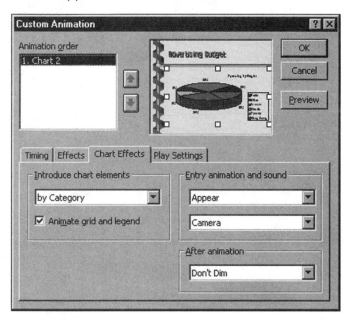

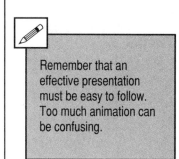

Remember that an effective presentation must be easy to follow. Too much animation can be confusing.

- **Play Settings tab** Allows you to adjust how audio and video clips will play during a slide show.

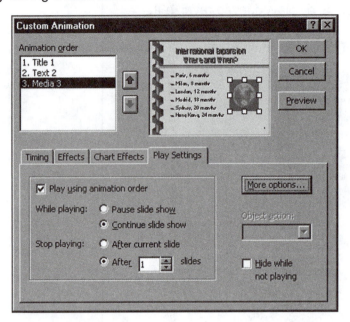

PowerPoint Central

- If you have access to the World Wide Web, you can go online and access web sites that offer templates, the latest tips, and information about PowerPoint. To access PowerPoint Central, click Tools, PowerPoint Central.

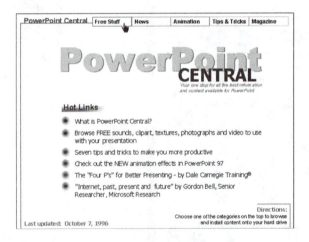

You must have your PowerPoint 97 software in your CD-ROM drive or be able to connect to the Internet in order to use PowerPoint Central.

- If you installed Office 97 from a CD-ROM, you can open the ValuPak to view the options that are available. Click on the option you want to explore. You can also go online and select from several hyperlinks to access information, audio and video clips, and other material that you can use in your presentations.

You can get free photos, clip art, and audio or video clips in PowerPoint Central, as well as advice on giving presentations and tips on how to use PowerPoint more effectively.

> *In this exercise, you will edit a previously created presentation by adding transition effects, builds, and timings to selected slides. You will then view your slide show.*

EXERCISE DIRECTIONS

1. Open ▥**VACATION**, or open ▤**15VACATI**.
2. Switch to Slide Sorter view.
3. Create a transition effect for each slide.
4. Add a five-second slide timing to slide 4.
5. Create an animation build for bulleted text on slides 2, 3, and 5 using any desired option.

   Optional: If you have Internet access, select PowerPoint Central from the Tools menu, select a Template, and apply it to all slides in the presentation.

6. Save the changes to the presentation; do not close the file.
7. View the slide show.
8. Print one copy of slide 4 in black and white.
9. Close the presentation window.

KEYSTROKES

✓ *Many of the following steps can be performed in other views, but all of the features are available in Slide view.*

APPLY PRESET ANIMATION TO TEXT, OBJECTS, OR CHARTS

Use Animation Effects Toolbar

1. Select slide containing list, object, or chart that you want to animate.
2. Click anywhere inside list, object, or chart that you want to animate.
3. Click desired animation effect on the toolbar.

Use Slide View

1. Select slide containing list, object, or chart that you want to animate.
2. Click **Sli̲de Show** .... `Alt`+`D`
3. Click **P̲reset Animation** .... `P`
4. Select desired effect . `↑` `↓`, `Enter`

   OR

   Click **O̲ff** .... `O`
   to turn off all effects.

TO PREVIEW ANIMATION

1. Click **Sli̲de Show** .... `Alt`+`D`
2. Click **Animation Pre̲view** .... `E`

A miniature of the slide with the selected build appears on screen.

APPLY CUSTOM ANIMATION TO LISTS

1. Select slide containing list, object, or chart that you want to animate.
2. Click anywhere inside list, object, or chart that you want to animate.
3. Click **Custom Animation** button .. 🖼 on Animation Effects toolbar.

   OR

   a. Click **Sli̲de Show** .... `Alt`+`D`
   b. Click **Custo̲m Animation** .... `M`

4. Select options for list, object, or chart that you want to animate:

   - **Animation o̲rder** .... `Alt`+`O`
     Select order for various elements to appear on slide.
   - **Timing** tab
     Select how, when, and/or if elements will be animated on slide.
   - **Effects** tab
     Select animation and sound effects.
   - **Chart Effects** tab
     Select how chart elements will be introduced on slide that contains a chart.
   - **Play Settings** tab
     Determine settings for audio and video clips on slide.

   ✓ *Options that are dimmed are not applicable to the currently selected item.*

NOTES

The Annotator

■ With the **Annotator** feature, you can draw on slides during a slide show. Annotations made on the screen during a slide show do not alter the slide in any way. Timings are suspended when you are annotating and begin again when you turn the Annotator off. Annotations are not permanent and disappear when you move to another slide.

■ The Annotator may be accessed by clicking on the Annotation button that appears in the lower-left corner of the screen during a slide show. Choose Pen from the pop-up menu. Your mouse then becomes a pencil point so you can write on the slide. To turn the Annotator off, click the button again and select Arrow from the pop-up menu.

■ To erase all annotations on the current slide, press the E key on the keyboard.

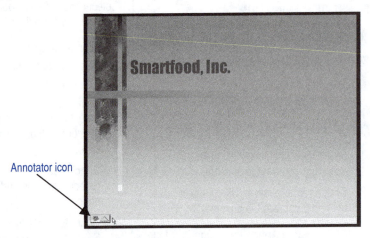

Annotator icon

To change the pen color:
- Right-click anywhere in the slide show.
- Click **Pointer Options**.
- Click **Pen Color**.
- Select a new color.

If the annotator button does not appear, move the mouse to display it. You can also right-click and select Pen from the Shortcut menu.

Create a Continuously Running Presentation

■ Timings must be set for each slide in a continuously running presentation to tell PowerPoint how long to display each slide. It is important to allow enough time for people to review the information presented on each slide when you set timings for a continuously running presentation.

■ To create a continuously running presentation, switch to Slide Sorter view, press Ctrl + A to select all slides. Then in the Slide Transition dialog box that follows, select Automatically and indicate the number of seconds you wish each slide to stay on screen.

■ A continuously running slide show can be stopped by pressing Esc.

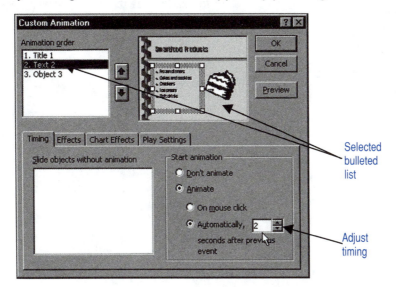

Selected bulleted list

Adjust timing

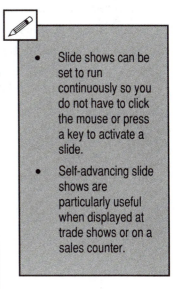

- Slide shows can be set to run continuously so you do not have to click the mouse or press a key to activate a slide.

- Self-advancing slide shows are particularly useful when displayed at trade shows or on a sales counter.

■ You can control the timing of individual elements on bulleted lists, objects, and charts in addition to regulating the timing of the entire slide. Adjust the time of individual elements on slides using the timing options in the Custom Animation dialog box.

> *In this exercise, you will edit a previously created presentation by adding transitions and a color scheme. You will also use the Annotator during your slide presentation.*

EXERCISE DIRECTIONS

1. Open 🖮WPRT, open 💾16WPRT.

2. Switch to Slide Sorter view.

3. Apply a transition effect and a transition speed for each slide in the presentation.

4. Apply a color scheme to the entire presentation.

5. Save the changes to the presentation.

6. View the slide show. Use the Annotator to underline each bulleted item on slide 2.

7. Change the advance method to advance automatically.

8. Set the slide show to run continuously and view the slide show again.

9. After viewing the entire presentation, stop the presentation.

10. Close the file; save the changes.

KEYSTROKES

ANNOTATE DURING SLIDE SHOWS

1. Open desired presentation and start slide show.
2. Click [🤚 △] in lower-left corner of screen to turn Annotator on.
3. Select **Pen** from pop-up menu.
4. Press left mouse button as you write on slide with "pencil."

   To turn Annotator off:

   a. Click [🤚 △] again.
   b. Select **Arrow**.

RUN SLIDE SHOW CONTINUOUSLY

1. Open desired presentation.
2. Click **Slide Show**.................[Alt]+[D]
3. Click **Slide Transition**...................[T]
4. Click **Automatically after # seconds**...................[Alt]+[C]
5. Enter number of seconds .... *number*
6. Click [Apply to All]..................[Alt]+[T]
7. Click **Slide Show**.................[Alt]+[D]
8. Click **Set Up Show**........................[S]
9. Click **Loop Continuously** ....[Alt]+[L] **until 'Esc'.**
10. Click [OK]..........................[Enter]

To stop continuous run of slide show:

Press **Esc** ....[Esc]

109

- Create Notes Pages and Handouts
- Notes Master and Handout Master ■ Format Notes Pages
- Prepare a Presentation for Viewing on Another Computer (Pack and Go)

NOTES

Create Notes Pages and Handouts

- The **Notes Pages** option prints your presentation showing a small image at the top of the page and a blank box (notes placeholder) below the image. You can enter reminders and/or additional information about the slide in the notes placeholder, or you can leave the box blank so that your audience can use it for notetaking when it is printed as a handout.

Notes pages are designed to be used by the speaker. They can contain both the slide and the text of a speech.

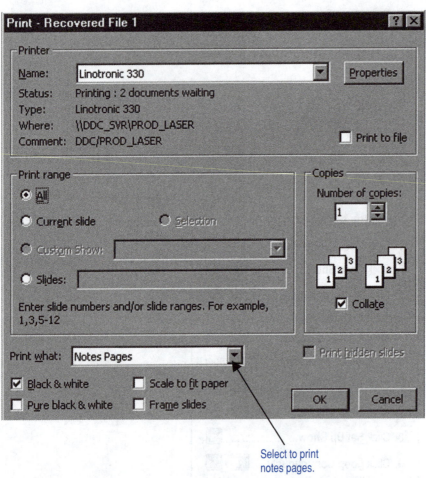

Select to print notes pages.

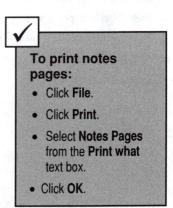

To print notes pages:

- Click **File**.
- Click **Print**.
- Select **Notes Pages** from the **Print what** text box.
- Click **OK**.

Notes Page View

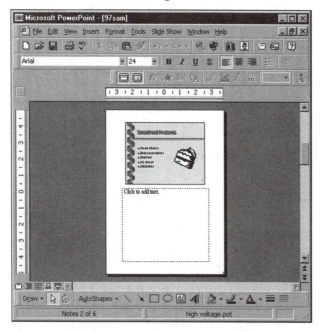

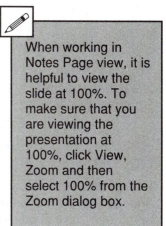

When working in Notes Page view, it is helpful to view the slide at 100%. To make sure that you are viewing the presentation at 100%, click View, Zoom and then select 100% from the Zoom dialog box.

■ To add notes to your slides, click the Notes Page View button 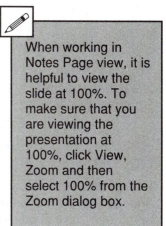 on the bottom left of your screen, or select <u>N</u>otes Page from the <u>V</u>iew menu. Then, enter the desired text in the notes placeholder.

Notes Master and Handout Master

■ In Exercise 10, you learned to use the slide master if you wanted to insert text or graphics on one slide (master) and have it appear on all slides of your presentation.

■ Using the notes master and the handout master also allows you to insert text and/or graphics on one page of your notes or handouts (master) and have it appear on all pages. Often, the time, date, and speaker's name are added to audience handouts.

■ Notes master and handout master may be accessed by selecting <u>M</u>aster, <u>N</u>otes Master or Han<u>d</u>out Master from the <u>V</u>iew menu.

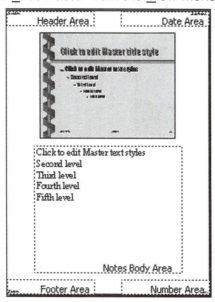

- The procedure to include the date, time, header and/or footer on the notes and handouts masters is the same as that used on the slide and title masters. *(See Exercise 10 for an explanation.)*

Format Notes Pages

- You can format text on the notes pages before or after you enter it. Use the commands on the Formatting toolbar, or all the commands (Font, Line Spacing, Bullet, etc.) on the Format menu.

Prepare a Presentation for Viewing on Another Computer (Pack and Go)

- Using **Pack and Go**, you can save a presentation that can be "unpacked" and viewed on another computer than the one you created it on. If the computer that will be used to view the presentation does not have PowerPoint installed on it, you can also have the PowerPoint Viewer stored with the presentation. This way, when the presentation is "unpacked" on the new computer, the presentation can be viewed. Using the **Pack and Go** feature, if linked files are used in a presentation, those files will also be stored with the presentation. *(Linking files will not be covered in this text.)*

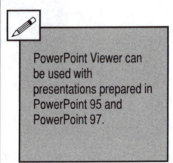

PowerPoint Viewer can be used with presentations prepared in PowerPoint 95 and PowerPoint 97.

- The **PowerPoint Viewer** is a program that lets you run slide shows created in PowerPoint on computers that do not have PowerPoint installed. The PowerPoint Viewer is available free and does not require a license. If you installed Office from a CD-ROM, you can find PowerPoint Viewer in the Office 97 ValuPack folder. The PowerPoint Viewer is also available from Microsoft on the World Wide Web.

- When you select Pack and Go from the File menu, the **Pack and Go Wizard** appears to walk you through preparing a presentation for viewing on another computer.

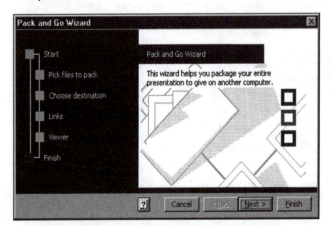

- Simply follow the Pack and Go Wizard steps to:
  - Pick the files to pack.
  - Select where you want to save the presentation, for example, to the A: drive.
  - Include files that are linked to the presentation.
  - Include PowerPoint Viewer, if the presentation will be used on a computer that does not have PowerPoint installed on it.

To view a presentation that has been packaged with Pack and Go:

- Use Windows Explorer to locate where the presentation is located, for example, on a disk in the A: drive.

- Double-click on 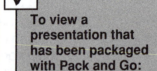 (Pack and Go Setup).

- Indicate where you want to copy the presentation.

- Double-click the PowerPoint Viewer (Ppview32).

- Click the presentation that you want to run.

In this exercise, you will add speaker's notes pages. You will also insert text in header and footer placeholders in Handout Master view. See Desired Results on pages 114 and 115.

EXERCISE DIRECTIONS

1. Open 🖥 **VACATION**, or open 💾 **17VACATI**.
2. Switch to Notes Page view.
3. Add the following notes to the notes placeholders. Use a 16-point, bold font:

   Slide 1

   - Introduce the company and yourself. Outline corporate history.

   Slide 2

   - Emphasize how important it is to get away from it all.

   Slide 3

   - A good workout may be just what the doctor ordered.

   Slide 4

   - It is never too late for a second honeymoon! Treat yourself to a weekend getaway.

   Slide 5

   - Meet people with common interests. Theme vacations include the great mystery book weekend and a ballroom dancing vacation.

   Slide 6

   - Everyone needs to feel special. At Globetrotters, we take care of everything so that you don't have to.

4. Switch to Notes Master view.
5. Insert the following text into the header placeholder (resize the placeholder to keep text on one line):

   - Presentation by Alonza Gomez of Globetrotters Travel.

6. Insert the following text into the Footer placeholder (resize the placeholder as needed):

   - Please call (718) 555-7654 to book your next trip.

7. Print one copy as Notes Pages.
8. Close the file; save the changes.

DESIRED RESULTS

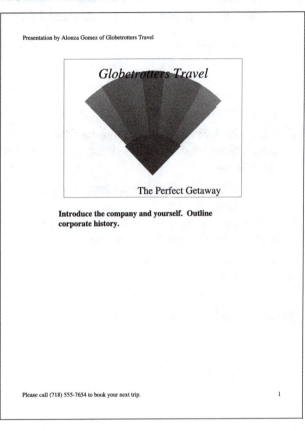

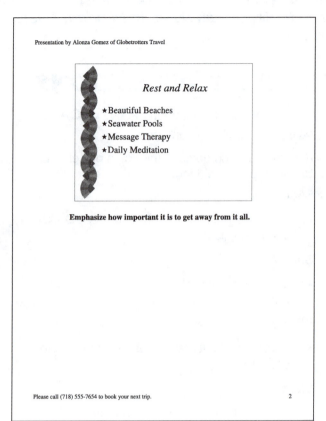

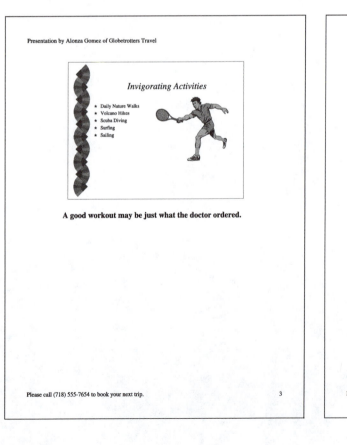

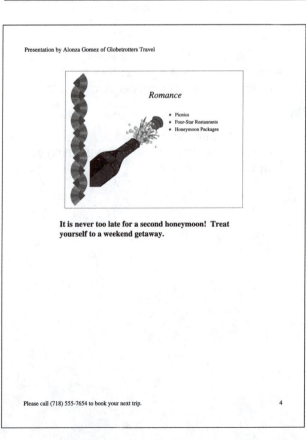

114

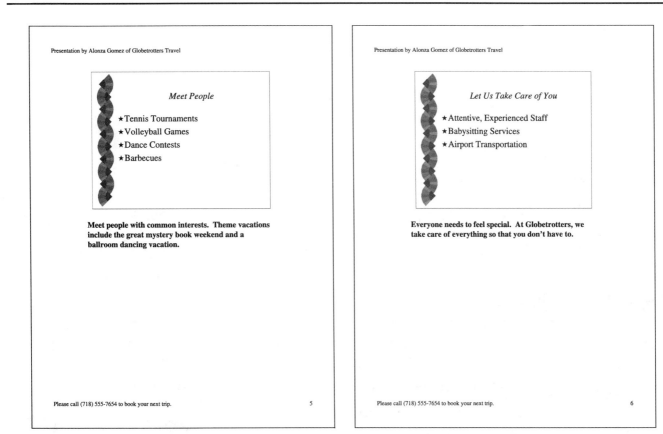

Presentation by Alonza Gomez of Globetrotters Travel

Meet People

★ Tennis Tournaments
★ Volleyball Games
★ Dance Contests
★ Barbecues

Meet people with common interests. Theme vacations include the great mystery book weekend and a ballroom dancing vacation.

Please call (718) 555-7654 to book your next trip.   5

Presentation by Alonza Gomez of Globetrotters Travel

Let Us Take Care of You

★ Attentive, Experienced Staff
★ Babysitting Services
★ Airport Transportation

Everyone needs to feel special. At Globetrotters, we take care of everything so that you don't have to.

Please call (718) 555-7654 to book your next trip.   6

KEYSTROKES

CREATE NOTES PAGES

1. Open desired presentation.
2. Click **Notes Page View** button......🖳

   OR

   a. Click **View**.....................`Alt`+`V`
   b. Click **Notes Page** ....`N`

   ✓ *To help legibility, remember to view notes pages at 100% zoom.*

3. Click on notes placeholder under slide miniature.
4. Type notes.

PRINT NOTES PAGES AND HANDOUTS

Ctrl + P

1. Open desired presentation.
2. Prepare notes pages.
3. Click **File**...............................`Alt`+`F`
4. Click **Print**.....................................`P`
5. Click **Print what** ....`Alt`+`W`,`↓` list arrow.
6. Select **Notes Pages** or **Handouts**.

   ✓ *As mentioned previously, handouts may be printed with 2, 3 or 6 slides per page.*

7. Select desired options, if necessary.
8. Click **OK** ....`Enter`

INSERT PAGE NUMBERS, DATE AND TIME, HEADERS OR FOOTERS

See **Keystrokes**, Exercise 10.

FORMAT TEXT ON NOTES PAGES

1. Enter text to format.

   OR
   Select text to format.

2. Click **Format**.......................`Alt`+`O` to apply desired format(s).

   OR
   Use buttons on Formatting toolbar to apply desired format(s).

FORMAT TEXT ON NOTES MASTER AND HANDOUT MASTER

1. Open a presentation or create a new one.
2. Click **View**............................`Alt`+`V`
3. Click **Master**................................`M`
4. Click **Notes Master**.........................`N`

   OR

   Click **Handout Master**.................`D`

5. Select placeholder to change formatting.
6. Use the text, drawing, and/or formatting tools, to create desired master layout.

   To see results:
   Click **Notes Page View** button........🖳

   OR

   a. Click **View** ....`Alt`+`V`
   b. Click **Notes Page**...................`N`

   ✓ *To see effect of additions to the handout master, print one copy of handouts with any number of slides per page.*

Next Exercise

■ Use Meeting Minder

NOTES

Use Meeting Minder

- The **Meeting Minder** displays a note window during your slide show to allow you to record notes, minutes, questions that arise during the show, or actions to be taken as a result of the discussion during the slide show.

- To access the Meeting Minder, start the slide show and select Meeting Minder from the Slide Show Shortcut menu. Minutes and action items can be recorded for every slide in the presentation, and you can access the Meeting Minder as often as you need. Information is stored until you complete the slide show.

- The Meeting Minder dialog box contains two tabs: Meeting Minutes and Action Items. Click on the desired tab.

- When you record items on the Action Items tab, PowerPoint adds a slide to the end of the presentation and tracks action items through the presentation so you can review them at the end of the slide show. After you type the description of the action and assign it to someone, click the Add button. Save the presentation to add the slide to the presentation file.

If you have Outlook 97 installed on your computer, you can click the Schedule button to schedule a meeting.

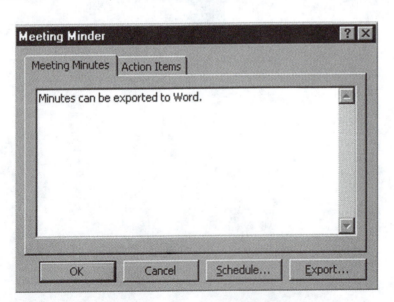

- If you have Microsoft Word installed on your system, items added to the Meeting Minder can be exported to Word. Word launches when you export the minutes and action items, and a predesigned page to include both categories appears. You can then use the page as you would any Word file.

- Minutes can also be exported to the Notes Pages of the presentation.

- To export notes, minutes, and action items from the Meeting Minder dialog box, access the Meeting Minder and click the Export button. Choose the Export option you wish to use and choose Export Now to send the information to its destination.

In this exercise, you will create a new presentation and export meeting minutes and action items to Microsoft Word. You will also create an Action Items slide.

EXERCISE DIRECTIONS

1. Begin a new presentation based on the **Ribbons** template.
2. Switch to Outline view.
3. Type the outline below:

Slide 1

Meeting Agenda

- North Shore Investment Club
- May 19, 1998

Slide 2

Minutes of Last Meeting

- Present: All active members present
- Portfolio Decisions
- Continue with Davis, Holmes & Co. as brokers

Slide 3

Portfolio Review

- Current standings of all holdings
- Current high/low performers
- Reports
  - Technology
  - Retail
  - Health Care
  - Energy
  - Media
  - Entertainment

Slide 4

Membership Issues

- Induct Beatrice Thomson as an official member.
- Annual dues need to be reviewed and possibly raised.

Slide 5

Research Committee Reports

- Technology
- Retail
- Health Care
- Energy
- Media
- Entertainment

Slide 6

- New Business

4. Switch to Slide Sorter view.
5. Apply the 2 column text AutoLayout to slide 3.
   - ✓ *Cut and paste three sub-bulleted items to the second column.*
6. Add transitions and animations as desired. Do not add timings.
7. Run the slide show after selecting manual advance in the Set Up Show dialog box.

8. Access Meeting Minder and insert the following comments where indicated:

Slide 2 (Minutes)

- (Meeting Minutes tab) All active members present.
- (Meeting Minutes tab) Inductee Beatrice Thomson also present.

Slide 5 (Research Committee Reports)

- (Meeting Minutes tab) Four annual reports due out in the next three weeks for Media committee.
- (Meeting Minutes tab) The newly-formed Entertainment committee will make first recommendations at the next meeting.
- (Action Items tab) Call brokers with sell order for all technology stocks not currently in the top ten performers. Assign the item to Jim.
- (Action Items tab) Call brokers with buy order for the health care stocks recommended by the committee. Assign the item to Jim.
- (Action Items tab) Media committee members should contact committee chair with preferred times for meeting regarding annual reports. Assign the item to Karen.

Slide 6 (New Business)

- (Meeting Minutes tab) Beatrice Thomson assigned to Health Care committee.
- (Action Items tab) Send all current membership materials to Beatrice Thomson. Assign the item to Timothy.

9. Note that a new slide (Action Items) has been appended to the end of the presentation.

10. Switch to Slide view.

11. Save the presentation; name it **MINUTES**.

    Optional: If you have Microsoft Word installed on your system, access Meeting Minder from the Tools menu and export the Meeting Minutes and Action Items to Word.

12. Print one copy of the Word document.

13. Close the document; name it **MINUTES**.

14. Exit Word; return to PowerPoint.

15. Close the presentation.

KEYSTROKES

USE MEETING MINDER TO CREATE MEETING MINUTES

1. Open presentation and start slide show.
2. Click *right* mouse button to display slide show shortcut menu.
3. Select **Meeting Minder**.
4. Click [Meeting Minutes].
5. Enter desired text.
6. Click **Schedule** .... `Alt`+`S`

   OR

   Click **Export** .... `Alt`+`E`

   OR

   Click **OK**.

USE MEETING MINDER TO CREATE ACTION ITEMS

1. Follow steps 1-3 at left.
2. Click **Action Items** tab.
3. Enter a **Description**
   of the item .... `Alt`+`C`
4. Note who the task was
   Assigned To .... `Alt`+`T`
5. Click **Add** .... `Alt`+`A`

   ✓ *PowerPoint will automatically create a slide listing all the Action Items and place it at the end of the presentation.*

6. To save Action Items slide, save the presentation after show is ended.

EXPORT FROM MEETING MINDER TO WORD

✓ *If Word is installed on your system, items added to the Meeting Minutes and Action Items tabs of the dialog box can be exported to Word. Word launches when you export the minutes and items.*

1. Add notes to Meeting Minder tabs during presentation.
2. Click **Tools** .... `Alt`+`T`
3. Click **Meeting Minder** .... `T`
4. Click **Export** .... `Alt`+`E`
5. Select the desired export option(s).
6. Click **Export Now** .... `Alt`+`E`
7. Edit Word document and save using standard procedures.

Exercise

19

■ **Summary**

In this exercise, you will open a presentation created in an earlier exercise, add animation, check styles, and run a slide show.

EXERCISE DIRECTIONS

1. Open ⌨**EFFECT**, or open 💾**19EFFECT**.

2. Switch to Slide Sorter view.

3. Animate the clip art on slide 3.

4. Animate all bulleted lists.

5. Use the Rehearse Timings feature to review the timings you have chosen. Make any needed adjustments.

6. Run the Style Checker. Make suggested changes as necessary.

7. Set up and run the slide show twice using slide timings and the Loop continuously until 'Esc' option.

8. Run the slide show again.

9. Access the Annotation feature to underline or circle the words on each slide that you think are most important.

10. Close the presentation; save the changes.

Exercise

20

■ **Summary**

In this exercise, you will open a previously created presentation, add slides, transitions, and access Meeting Minder.

EXERCISE DIRECTIONS

1. Open ⌨**WPRT**, or open 💾**20WPRT**.

2. Add a new slide (The Fall Forecast) after slide 7. Use the Bulleted Text AutoLayout.

3. Add the following bulleted text to the slide:

   The Fall Forecast
   - New shows are in the works
   - New sales strategies are being developed
   - Expect the best season yet!

4. Add a Checkerboard Across transition to the new slide and set the timing to six seconds.

5. Add a new slide (New Sales Strategies) after slide 8 using the Clip Art & Text AutoLayout. Add an appropriate clip art.

6. Add the following text to the slide. Adjust the text so each bulleted item fits on one line and the line spacing is balanced.

   New Sales Strategies
   - Incentive Programs
   - Flexible Contracts
   - New Presentation Materials
   - More Sales Support

7. Add a Blinds Vertical transition with an eight second timing to the new slide.

8. Run the slide show using slide timings. Turn the Loop option off.

9. Access Meeting Minder and insert Minutes and Action Items as follows:

   Slide 4 (Programming Projections) - Minutes
   - Our programming projections brought in much more revenue than our programs replaced lost.
   - We anticipate an increase of 20% in funding for new shows.

   Slide 9 (New Sales Strategies) - Minutes
   - We will cover these new strategies in depth during this afternoon's session.

   Slide 10 (The Year In Review) - Action Items
   - Organizational Changes will be assigned to Jim.
   - Sales Records will be assigned to Angeline.
   - Ratings Review will be assigned to Fran Conte.

10. Run the slide show again using manual advance.

    Optional: If you have Microsoft Word installed, export Minutes and Action Items to a Word document.

11. Print one copy of the new Word document.

12. Close the presentation; save the changes.

Next
Lesson

Lesson 4

Charts and Tables
Exercises 21-25

- Insert a Chart

- Insert an Organizational Chart Slide

- Insert a Table

- Insert and Delete Columns and Rows

- Change Column widths

- Create an Excel Worksheet on a Slide

■ **Insert a Chart**

Chart Toolbar

View Datasheet

Chart Type

NOTES

Insert a Chart

- A chart may be added to a PowerPoint slide by importing one that was already created in Excel, or by using the Chart feature in PowerPoint to create one.

- To create a chart in PowerPoint, double-click the chart placeholder on any AutoLayout includes a chart.

Text and Chart AutoLayout Slide

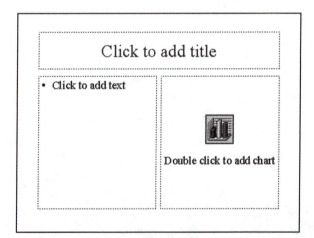

Click to add title

• Click to add text

Double click to add chart

PowerPoint charts are created in MS Graph, a program that comes with Office 97. MS Graph must be installed for the chart feature to work.

A chart may be added to a PowerPoint slide by importing one that was already created in Excel, or by using the Chart slide in PowerPoint to create a new one.

- To insert a chart without using a placeholder, select <u>C</u>hart from the <u>I</u>nsert menu, or click the Insert Chart button ▦ on the Standard toolbar.

- A datasheet window displays (see next page) along with a Chart toolbar (see above) that replaces the Standard toolbar. Several charting features will also appear on the Formatting toolbar.

■ Delete the sample data in the datasheet and enter the data you wish to chart. The chart will reflect the new data. Click on the slide (not the chart) to hide the datasheet. To see the datasheet again, double-click the chart.

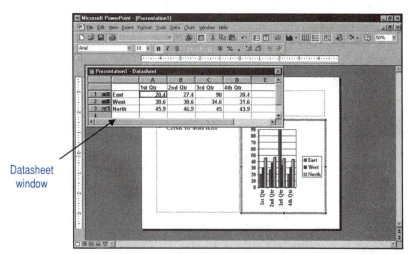

Datasheet
window

■ The default chart type is 3-D Column. However, you may change the chart type before or after you enter data in the datasheet by clicking the chart on the slide, selecting Chart Type from the Chart menu, and then selecting either the Standard Types or Custom Types tab from the Chart Type dialog box.

Chart Type Dialog Box

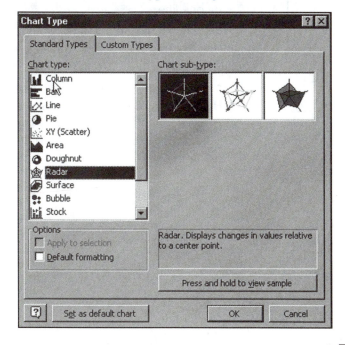

■ You can also click the list arrow next to the Chart Type button 📊▾ on the Chart toolbar, and then select one of the chart types from the choices on the drop-down palette that appears.

■ You may enhance your chart with a title and/or data labels. Data labels allow you to indicate the exact value of each data point. Follow the procedures outlined in the Keystrokes section on page 130 to insert and edit a chart title and data labels.

- You can also rotate and change the elevation of 3-D (three dimensional) graphs so that they present a different angle of the data. To do so, select the chart. Then, select 3-D View from the Chart menu. The preview area within the 3-D View dialog box displays the changes on the graph angle. Click Apply to apply the selected 3-D changes to your chart.
- You can resize and move a chart just like any other object.

In this exercise, you will create a new presentation which includes two chart slides.

EXERCISE DIRECTIONS

1. Create a new presentation based on the Professional template.

2. Insert a Title Slide and a Bulleted List slide. Enter the text shown in slides 1 and 2 of the Desired Result.

3. Insert a Text & Clip Art slide. Insert the text and clip art shown in slide 3.

4. Insert a Chart & Text slide. Enter the title and text shown in slide 4.

5. Enter the following chart data:

	3-Jun	10-Jun	17-Jun	24-Jun
Mutual Funds	21.4	28.1	91.1	20.5
Stocks	31.2	37.4	33.9	30.9
401 (k) Plan	46.1	46.7	44.9	42.9

6. Accept the default 3-D column chart.

7. Insert a Chart slide. Enter the title "A Suggested Budget."

8. Create a pie chart using the following data:

	Housing	Transportation	Food/ Clothing	Debt Payment	Savings
BUDGET	35	20	20	15	10

9. Insert data labels to show percent.

   IMPORTANT: See the keystrokes for the procedure for inserting labels.

10. Resize the legend, if necessary, so that entries fit on one line.

11. Switch to Slide Sorter view. Compare your results to those in the illustration.

12. Spell check.

13. Print one copy as Handouts (6 slides per page) in Black and White.

14. Close the presentation; save it as **INVEST**.

DESIRED RESULTS

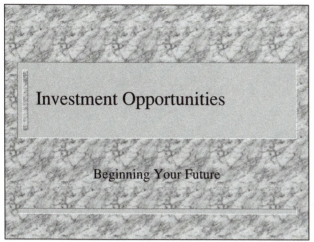

SLIDE 1

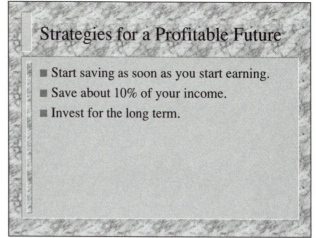

SLIDE 2

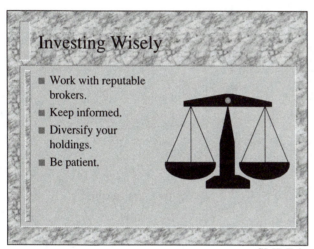

SLIDE 3

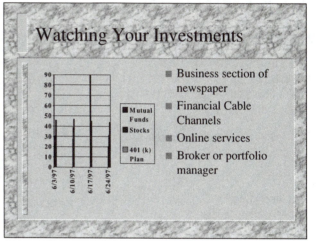

SLIDE 4

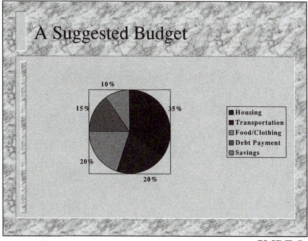

SLIDE 5

KEYSTROKES

INSERT A CHART ON A SLIDE

1. Select a slide containing a Chart placeholder from Slide Layout and double-click the chart placeholder.

   OR

   Click **Insert** .... Alt + I , H
   and select **Chart**.

   OR

   Click **Insert Chart** button .... 📊
   on the Standard toolbar.

2. Delete the sample data and enter the data you wish to chart in the datasheet.

   To delete data in a Datasheet:

   a. Press **Ctrl + A** .... Ctrl + A

   b. Press **Delete** .... Del

3. Click the graph to hide the datasheet.

   OR

   Click **View Datasheet** button .... 🔲

Select a chart type:

1. Click **Chart** .... Alt + C

2. Select **Chart Type** .... T

3. Select either the Standard types tab or the Custom types tab.

4. Select desired **Chart type** ..... Alt + C

5. Select desired
   Chart sub-type .... Alt + T

6. Click **OK** .... Enter

Insert a Title:

1. Click **Chart** .... Alt + C

2. Click **Chart Options** .... O

3. Click **Titles** tab.

4. Click **Chart title** .... Alt + T

5. Type title .... *title*

6. Click **Category (X) axis** .... Alt + C

7. Type title for x axis .... *title*

8. Click **Value (Y) axis** .... Alt + V

9. Type title for y axis .... *title*

10. Click **OK** .... Enter

Color Chart Title:

1. Right-click Chart Title.

2. Click **Format Chart Title** .... Alt + O

3. Click **Font** tab .... F

4. Click **Color** .... Alt + C

5. Select desired color.

6. Click **OK** .... Enter

Insert Data Labels:

1. Click **Chart** .... Alt + C

2. Click **Chart Options** .... Alt + O

3. Click **Data Labels** tab .... D

4. Select desired label type.

5. Click **OK** .... Enter

Change legend position:

1. Click **Chart** .... Alt + C

2. Click **Chart Options** .... O

3. Click **Legend** tab.

4. Select desired placement option.

   To hide the legend:

   Deselect the **Show legend** ... Alt + S
   check box.

5. Click **OK** .... Enter

CHANGE FONT

1. Right-click chart item to be changed.

2. Click **Format Legend** .... O
   or **Format Axis**.

3. Click **Font** tab .... Ctrl + Tab

4. Select desired font options.

5. Click **OK** .... Enter

Next
Exercise

■ Insert an Organization Chart Slide

Chart Toolbar

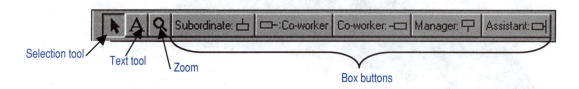

Selection tool   Text tool   Zoom

Box buttons

NOTES

Insert an Organization Chart Slide

■ An **Organization Chart** is used to illustrate a company's hierarchy or structure.

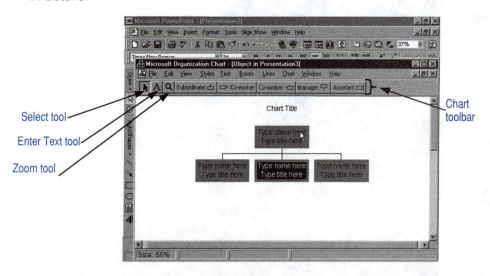

Select tool

Enter Text tool

Zoom tool

Chart toolbar

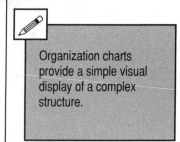

Organization charts provide a simple visual display of a complex structure.

■ Organization charts may also be used to show the flow of a project or a family tree.

■ PowerPoint contains an Organization Chart AutoLayout. To create an organization chart, select the Organization Chart AutoLayout and double-click on the organization chart placeholder.

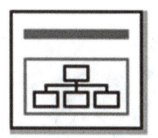

- By default, four boxes display. However, you can attach additional boxes to existing boxes and rearrange boxes. In addition, you can format each box with different fonts, font sizes, fill colors, and borders, and text alignments.

- There are four types of boxes: Subordinate, Co-Worker, Manager, and Assistant. Each box type attaches to the existing boxes differently. Note the box shapes available on the Chart icon bar.

- You can also rearrange boxes. To do so, click the box you wish to move and select Cut from the Edit menu. Then, click in the box to which you wish to attach the cut box and select Paste from the Edit menu.

- You can enter up to four lines of text in each box. As you type, the box will adjust its size to fit the text.

- After you have added the desired boxes and entered the desired text, select Close and Return to Presentation from the File menu.

> *In this exercise, you will insert an organization chart and a chart slide to a previously created presentation.*

EXERCISE DIRECTIONS

1. Open ⌨**SWITZERLAND**, or open 💾**22SWIT**. Display slide 7, Government, in Slide view.

2. Delete the bullet points. Reformat the slide using the Organization Chart AutoLayout.

3. Enter the chart information shown on slide 7 of the Desired Result and format it as follows:
   - Delete the top box.
   - Add a subordinate to the middle box. Add a co-worker to the subordinate.
   - Change the color of the font for all boxes to red.
   - Change the box line style, shadow style, and color for all boxes as desired.

4. Update the slide and exit the Microsoft Organization Chart application.

5. After slide 3, insert a new chart slide. Enter the slide title: Resource Distribution.

6. Create a 3-D pie chart using the following data:

	Mountains	Forests	Water
Resources	70	25	5

7. Insert data labels. Show percent.

8. Show Legend key, if not visible.

9. Run slide show and compare your presentation with the Desired Result.

10. Make any necessary changes.

11. Print one copy as Handouts with six slides per page.

12. Close the file; save the changes.

SLIDE 1

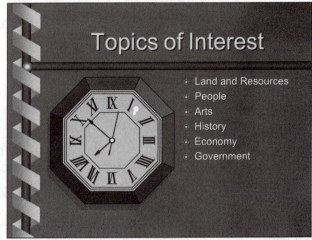

SLIDE 2

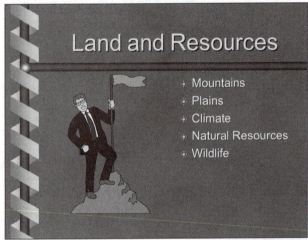

SLIDE 3

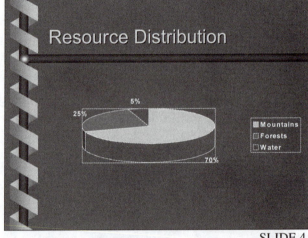

SLIDE 4

SLIDE 5

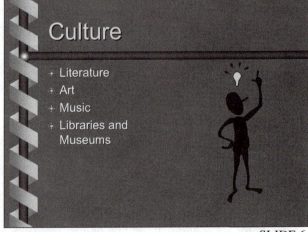

SLIDE 6

Continued…

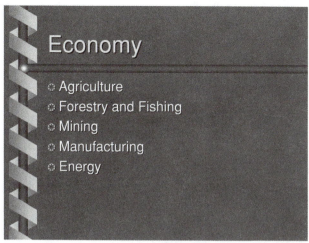

SLIDE 7

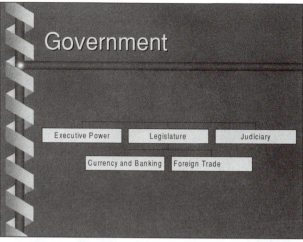

SLIDE 8

SLIDE 9

KEYSTROKES

CREATE ORGANIZATION CHART ON AUTOLAYOUT SLIDE

1. Select the AutoLayout slide containing the Organization Chart placeholder.
2. Enter the title in the title placeholder.
3. Double-click the organization chart placeholder.
4. Select a box.
5. Type name and press **Enter**.
6. Type title and press **Enter**.
7. Type comment(s), if desired, and press **Enter**.
8. Click another box and repeat steps 5-7.

   OR

   Click outside the organization box to close box.
9. Click **File**..............................Alt + F
10. Click **Close and Return**................C
    to [*Presentation*].

INSERT BOX

1. Click the appropriate button for the type of box tool you wish to attach.
2. Click existing box to which you wish to attach new one.

REARRANGE BOXES

1. Select the box to be moved.
2. Position mouse pointer on border of box to be moved.
3. Drag box to new location.
4. Release mouse button.

- **Insert a Table** ■ **Insert and Delete Columns and Rows**
- **Change Column Widths** ■ **Create an Excel Worksheet on a Slide**

Standard Toolbar

Insert Microsoft
Word Table

Insert Microsoft
Excel Worksheet

NOTES

Insert a Table

- A Table may be added to a PowerPoint slide by importing one that was created in Microsoft Word, or by using the Table feature in PowerPoint to create one.
- To create a Table on a slide, double-click a table placeholder on a Table AutoLayout slide.

Table AutoLayout Slide

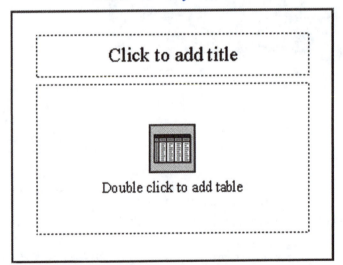

Click to add title

Double click to add table

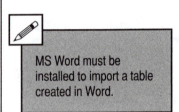

MS Word must be installed to import a table created in Word.

- To insert a table without using a placeholder, click the Insert Word Table button ⊞ on the Standard toolbar, or select Microsoft Word <u>T</u>able from the <u>P</u>icture submenu on the <u>I</u>nsert menu. PowerPoint offers one AutoLayout slide containing a table format.
- After double-clicking the table placeholder or selecting <u>P</u>icture, Microsoft Word <u>T</u>able from the <u>I</u>nsert menu, the Insert Word Table dialog box displays for you to indicate how many <u>c</u>olumns and <u>r</u>ows you need for your table.

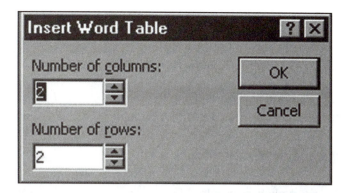

- If you are using the Insert Microsoft Word Table button [icon] on the Standard toolbar, you can drag the mouse across the grid to indicate the number of rows and columns you desire.

- Once you have selected the number of rows and columns, a table displays on your slide, and PowerPoint's toolbars and Menu are temporarily replaced by Word's toolbars and Menu bar. This enables you to use Word's table editing features inside PowerPoint.

- Click in a cell and enter the desired text. Press the Tab key to move the insertion point from cell to cell.

- After you have entered all table text, click on the slide containing the table to return to PowerPoint, or press Escape. You can return to the table and make changes at any time by double-clicking inside the table.

- If you use a Table AutoLayout slide to insert your table, the columns and rows will be evenly spaced within the table placeholder. You can also adjust the column widths if you choose *(see Change Column Width, in this exercise)*.

- If you create your table on a slide not containing a table placeholder and use the grid to create the columns and rows, you may need to reposition or resize the table on the slide. To reposition the table, click within the table and drag it to the desired position. To resize a table, drag a handle. You may also need to adjust column widths *(see Change Column Width, in this exercise)*.

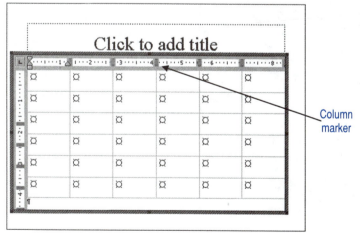

Column marker

Insert and Delete Columns and Rows

- To insert a row, select Insert Rows from the Table menu or right-click a cell and select Insert Rows. A new row will be inserted above the insertion point position.

- To insert a column, highlight the column to the right of the column to be inserted. Then, select Insert Columns from the Table menu or right-click and select Insert Columns.

- To delete a column, highlight the column to be deleted, right-click and select Delete Columns.

- To delete a row, click in the row to delete, right-click and select Delete Cells. In the Delete Cells dialog box that follows, select Delete entire row.

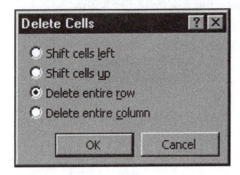

Change Column Width

- To adjust column widths and see the immediate effect of the change on the table as it is being made, position the mouse pointer on the column marker. When the mouse pointer changes to a double-headed arrow, press and hold the mouse as you drag the column marker left or right to the desired width or table size.

- You can also adjust column widths and margins within the table using a specific measurement. Select Cell Height and Width from the Table menu. In the Cell Height and Width dialog box that follows, click the Column tab and type the desired measurement in the Width box.

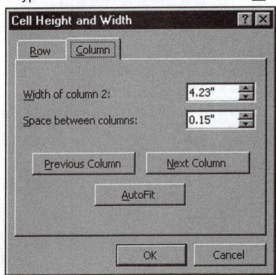

 Column width may be changed using a specific measurement or by dragging the column marker located on the Ruler in the Table to the desired width.

Table AutoFormat

■ The AutoFormat feature within Microsoft Word provides predefined formatting styles to apply to your table.

■ Select Table Auto<u>F</u>ormat from the <u>T</u>able menu to access AutoFormat. In the Table AutoFormat dialog box that follows, available styles are listed on the left, and a preview window displays the selected style on the right. Click OK to apply the selected format to your table.

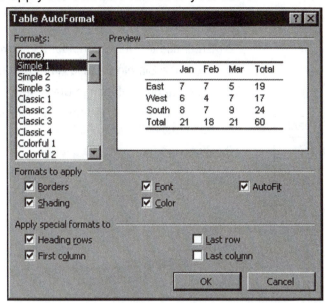

Create an Excel Worksheet

■ If you have office 97 on your computer, you can create an Excel worksheet on a slide. To create an Excel worksheet on a slide, click the Insert Microsoft Excel Worksheet button on the Standard toolbar. A drop-down grid appears as it did with tables. Click and drag across and down the grid to indicate how many columns and rows you desire in your worksheet. When you release your mouse, a worksheet appears, ready for you to enter data. PowerPoint's Standard toolbar is temporarily replaced by Excel's toolbar and menu.

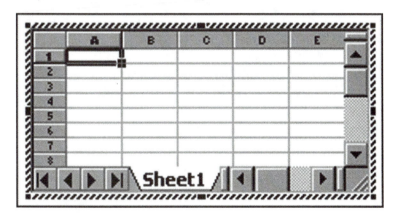

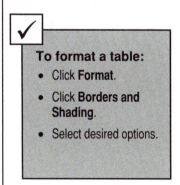

To format a table:
- Click **Format**.
- Click **Borders and Shading**.
- Select desired options.

EXERCISE DIRECTIONS

1. Open ⌨**INVEST**, or open 💾**23INVEST**

2. Display slide 4, Watching Your Investment.

3. Insert a new Table AutoLayout slide.

4. Select the table placeholder.

5. Create a table with 4 columns and 4 rows.

6. Enter the following table data:

Investment Type	1 Year	3 Years	5 Years
Income	5.51%	5.32%	5.03%
Capital Growth	22.59%	18.95%	14.71%
Long-Term Capital Growth	12.41%	6.32%	10.16%

7. Adjust column widths and row heights so text appears as in the illustration.

8. Enter title text in placeholder as shown.

9. Apply the Simple 3 Table AutoFormat to the table.

10. View the presentation in Black and White view.

11. Print one copy as Handouts with six slides per page in black and white.

12. Close the file; save the changes.

DESIRED RESULTS

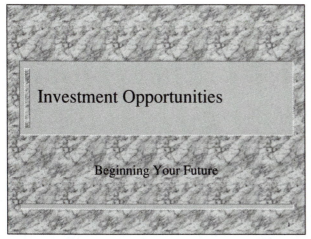

SLIDE 1

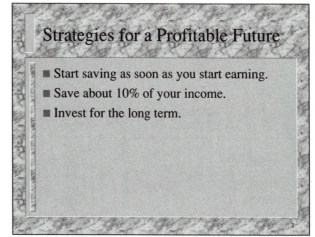

SLIDE 2

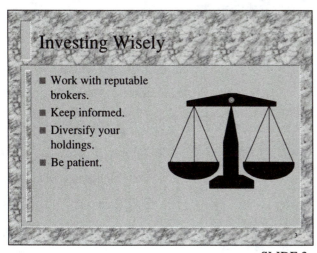

SLIDE 3

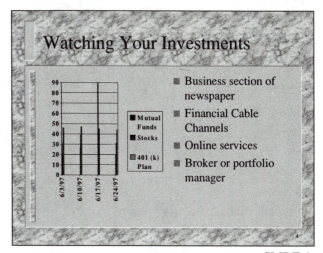

SLIDE 4

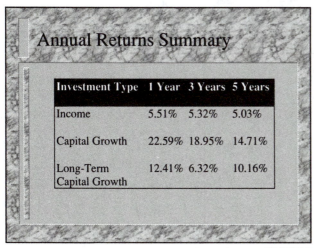

SLIDE 5

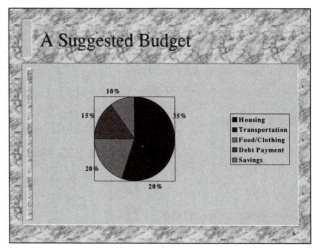

SLIDE 6

KEYSTROKES

INSERT A TABLE ON A SLIDE

1. Select a slide layout containing a table placeholder.
2. Enter the title in the title placeholder.
3. Double-click the table placeholder.
4. Enter desired
   Number of columns..............`Alt`+`C`
5. Enter desired
   Number of rows ....`Alt`+`R`
6. Click **OK**......................................`Enter`
7. Click the first cell and enter desired text.
8. Press **Tab** ....`Tab`
   to advance to the next cell.
   OR
   Press **Shift** + **Tab** ....`Shift`+`Tab`
   to move to the previous cell.
9. Click on slide to insert table and return to PowerPoint.
   OR

To insert a table without using a placeholder:

1. Click the **Insert Microsoft Word Table** button ▦ on the Standard toolbar and drag to highlight desired number of columns and rows.
   OR
   a. Click **Insert** ....`Alt`+`I`
   b. Click **Picture**............................`P`
   c. Click **Microsoft Word Table** .....`T`
   d. Enter desired
      Number of columns ....`Alt`+`C`
   e. Enter desired
      Number of rows..............`Alt`+`R`
   f. Click **OK**..............................`Enter`

2. Click the first cell and enter desired text.
3. Press **Tab** ....`Tab`
   to advance to the next cell.
   OR
   Press **Shift** + **Tab** ....`Shift`+`Tab`
   to move to the previous cell.
4. Click on slide to insert table and return to PowerPoint.

INSERT COLUMNS/ROWS

COLUMNS

1. Double-click the table in PowerPoint.
2. Select the column to the right of the new column you wish to insert.
   OR
   a. Click in the cell to the right of the new column you wish to insert.
   b. Click **Table**......................`Alt`+`A`
   c. Click **Select Column** ....`C`
3. Click **Table** ....`Alt`+`A`
4. Click **Insert Columns**....................`I`

ROWS

1. Double-click the table in PowerPoint.
2. Click in the cell below the new row you wish to insert.
3. Click **Table** ....`Alt`+`A`
4. Click **Insert Rows** ....`I`

DELETE COLUMNS/ROWS

1. Double-click the table in PowerPoint.
2. Select the columns or rows to delete.
3. Click **Table** ....`Alt`+`A`
4. Click **Delete Columns**....................`D`
   OR
   Click **Delete Rows** ....`D`

CHANGE COLUMN WIDTH

1. Double-click the table on the slide.
2. Select the column for which you want to change the width.
3. Click **Table** ....`Alt`+`A`
4. Click **Cell Height and Width**..........`W`
5. Click the **Column** tab ....`Alt`+`C`
6. Click the **Width** text box ....`Alt`+`W`
7. Type new width.........................*number*
   OR
   Click arrow buttons to change width incrementally.
8. Click **OK** ....`Enter`

TABLE AUTOFORMAT

1. Double-click the table in PowerPoint.
2. Click **Table** ....`Alt`+`A`
3. Click **Table AutoFormat**...............`F`
4. Make desired changes.
5. Click **OK** ....`Enter`

Next
Exercise

■ Summary

In this exercise, you will edit a previously created presentation, adding an organization chart and a data chart.

EXERCISE DIRECTIONS:

1. Open ⌨**VACATION**, or open 💾**24VACATI**.

2. Display slide 2, Rest and Relax, in Slide view.

3. Reformat slide 2 using the 2 Column Text AutoLayout, and distribute the bulleted items between the two columns.

4. Insert a new slide after slide 6, Let Us Take Care of You. Use the Organization Chart AutoLayout and insert the text shown in Illustration A.

   ✓ *If you do not have the Organization Chart component of PowerPoint installed, you may format this slide as a Bulleted List and use different level bullets for the information shown.*

5. Insert a new chart slide after slide 12. Add the title shown in Illustration B.

6. Enter the following data:

	to $5,000	to $10,000	to $15,000	to $20,000
SAVINGS	0%	2%	5%	7.5%

7. Use the first Area option as the chart type.

8. Spell check and run slide show.

9. Print one copy as handouts with six slides per page in black and white.

10. Close the file; save the changes.

ILLUSTRATION A

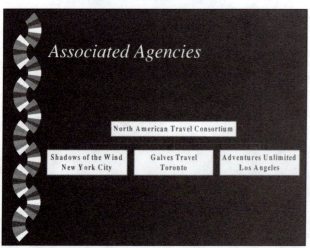

ILLUSTRATION B

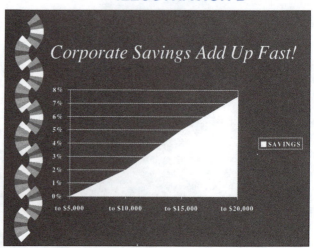

Exercise 25

■ Summary

In this exercise, you will reformat a slide using a table AutoLayout, and you will change the font color and size, and center-align all row and column headings.

EXERCISE DIRECTIONS

1. Open 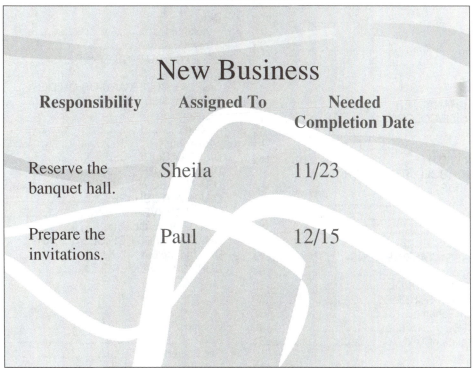MINUTES, or open 25MINUTES.
2. Switch to Slide view, if necessary.
3. Move to slide 6, New Business.
4. Reformat the slide using a table AutoLayout.
5. Change the heading and insert the table text as shown in Illustration A.
6. Use a 26-point bold font for all column headers. Change the font to pink.
7. Use a 26-point bold font for all row headers. Change the font to blue.
8. Use a 32-point fuschia font for the table text.
9. Center the headings.
10. Verify that all headings are centered.
11. Switch to Slide view.
12. Print one copy as Handouts with three slides per page.
13. Close the file; save the changes.

ILLUSTRATION A

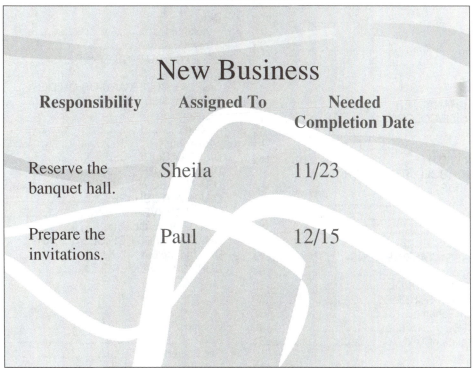

	New Business	
Responsibility	**Assigned To**	**Needed Completion Date**
Reserve the banquet hall.	Sheila	11/23
Prepare the invitations.	Paul	12/15

Index

Note: Entries in all capital letters indicate keystroke procedures.

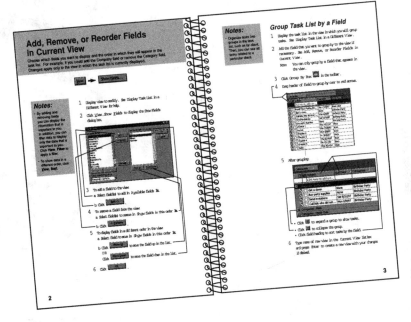

More Fast-teach Learning Books

Did we make one for you?

Title	Cat. No.
Corel WordPerfect 7 for Win 95	Z12
DOS 5–6.2 (Book & Disk)	D9
DOS + Windows	Z7
Excel 5 for Windows	E9
Excel 7 for Windows 95	XL7
INTERNET	Z15
Lotus 1-2-3 Rel. 2.2–4.0 for DOS	L9
Lotus 1-2-3 Rel. 4 & 5 for Windows	B9
Microsoft Office	M9
Microsoft Office for Windows 95	Z6
Windows 3.1 – A Quick Study	WQS-1
Windows 95	Z3
Word 2 for Windows	K9
Word 6 for Windows	1-WDW6
Word 7 for Windows 95	Z10
WordPerfect 5.0 & 5.1 for DOS	W9
WordPerfect 6 for DOS	P9
WordPerfect 6 for Windows	Z9
WordPerfect 6.1 for Windows	H9
Works 3 for Windows	1-WKW3
Works 4 for Windows 95	Z8

DESKTOP PUBLISHING LEARNING BOOKS

Word 6 for Windows	Z2
WordPerfect 5.1 for DOS	WDB
WordPerfect 6 for Windows	F9
WordPerfect 6.1 for Windows	Z5

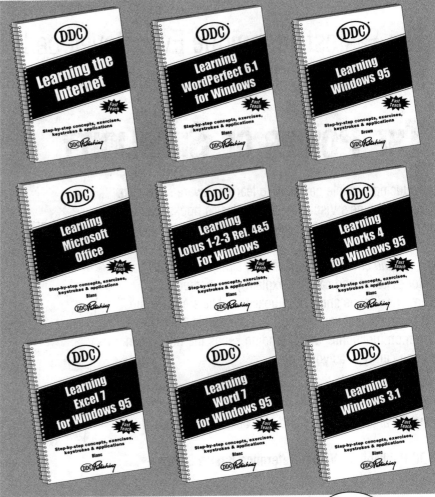

New One-Day Courses

Title	Cat. No.	Title	Cat. No.
Access 7 for Win 95	**DC-1**	**Netscape Navigator**	**DC-10**
Access 97	**DC-2**	**& Simulation**	
Excel 7 for Win 95	**DC-3**	**Outlook 97**	**DC-11**
Excel 97	**DC-4**	**PageMaker 5**	**DC-12**
Internet E-Mail & FTP	**DC-5**	**PowerPoint 7 for Win**	**DC-13**
Simulation		**PowerPoint 97**	**DC-14**
Intro to Computers	**DC-6**	**Windows NT 3.5**	**DC-15**
Macintosh Sys. 7.5	**DC-7**	**Word 7 for Win 95**	**DC-17**
MS Explorer	**DC-8**	**Word 97**	**DC-18**
& Simulation		**WordPerfect 6.1**	**DC-19**
MS Project 4	**DC-9**	**Visual Basics 3.0**	**DC-20**

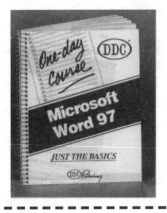

DDC can't promise you will master your software with these books, but you will be using it the very next day. These books are great for instructor-led one-day workshops or seminars. They are also ideal for the home computer owner or student who wants to get up and running with software . . . fast.

- - - - - - - - - - - - - - - **ORDER FORM** - - - - - - - - - - - - - - -

DDC Publishing   275 Madison Ave. NY, NY 10016 $**22** ea.

QTY.	CAT. NO.	TITLE

☐ Check enclosed. Add $2.50 for post. & handling & $1.50 for ea. additional. guide. NY State res. add local sales tax.

☐ VISA   ☐ Mastercard   *100% Refund Guarantee*

No._____ Exp._____

Name_____

Firm _____

Address_____

City, State, Zip _____

Phone (800)528-3897   Fax (800)528-3862

SEE OUR COMPLETE CATALOG ON THE INTERNET
http://www.ddcpub.com

FREE CATALOG
AND
UPDATED LISTING

We don't just have books that find your answers faster; we also have books that teach you how to use your computer without the fairy tales and the gobbledygook.

We also have books to improve your typing, spelling and punctuation.

Return this card for a free catalog and mailing list update.

275 Madison Avenue,
New York, NY 10016

☐ Please send me your catalog
and put me on your mailing list.

_____
Name

_____
Firm (if any)

_____
Address

_____
City, State, Zip

Phone (800) 528-3897   Fax (800) 528-3862

SEE OUR COMPLETE CATALOG ON THE INTERNET @: http://www.ddcpub.com

---

FREE CATALOG
AND
UPDATED LISTING

We don't just have books that find your answers faster; we also have books that teach you how to use your computer without the fairy tales and the gobbledygook.

We also have books to improve your typing, spelling and punctuation.

Return this card for a free catalog and mailing list update.

275 Madison Avenue,
New York, NY 10016

☐ Please send me your catalog
and put me on your mailing list.

_____
Name

_____
Firm (if any)

_____
Address

_____
City, State, Zip

Phone (800) 528-3897   Fax (800) 528-3862

SEE OUR COMPLETE CATALOG ON THE INTERNET @: http://www.ddcpub.com

---

FREE CATALOG
AND
UPDATED LISTING

We don't just have books that find your answers faster; we also have books that teach you how to use your computer without the fairy tales and the gobbledygook.

We also have books to improve your typing, spelling and punctuation.

Return this card for a free catalog and mailing list update.

DDC *Publishing*

275 Madison Avenue,
New York, NY 10016

☐ Please send me your catalog
and put me on your mailing list.

_____
Name

_____
Firm (if any)

_____
Address

_____
City, State, Zip

Phone (800) 528-3897   Fax (800) 528-3862

SEE OUR COMPLETE CATALOG ON THE INTERNET @: http://www.ddcpub.com

BUSINESS REPLY MAIL

FIRST CLASS MAIL   PERMIT NO. 7321   NEW YORK, N.Y.

POSTAGE WILL BE PAID BY ADDRESSEE

275 Madison Avenue
New York, NY 10157-0410

NO POSTAGE
NECESSARY
IF MAILED
IN THE
UNITED STATES

BUSINESS REPLY MAIL

FIRST CLASS MAIL   PERMIT NO. 7321   NEW YORK, N.Y.

POSTAGE WILL BE PAID BY ADDRESSEE

275 Madison Avenue
New York, NY 10157-0410

NO POSTAGE
NECESSARY
IF MAILED
IN THE
UNITED STATES

BUSINESS REPLY MAIL

FIRST CLASS MAIL   PERMIT NO. 7321   NEW YORK, N.Y.

POSTAGE WILL BE PAID BY ADDRESSEE

275 Madison Avenue
New York, NY 10157-0410

NO POSTAGE
NECESSARY
IF MAILED
IN THE
UNITED STATES